APOSTOLIC PRAYERS THAT EVOKE HEAVEN'S SWIFT RESPONSE TO MAJOR SPIRITUAL ATTACKS

RAPID FIRE

EBENEZER & ABIGAIL GABRIELS

Ebenezer Gabriel Books

USA

Ebenezer Gabriels Publishing

www.ebenezergabriels.org

Paperback Published March 2018
Hardcover Published March 2022

Rapid Fire is the story documenting the powers of technical prayers. Documented by two missionaries, sent on a special mission to build worship altars for the Lord.

Rapid Fire offers believer-tested biblical methods of effective and apostolic prayers to combat spiritual attacks, which seek to shut the doors against your life's calling. Rapid Fire book was birthed forth at the onset of God's move in the earlier days of our Prophetic and Apostolic ministry. It is a book powered by God's covenant of rapid activation of deliverance from evil attacks and prosperity in offensive battles. Rapid Fire is a prayer resource to bring into the offensive battlefront to defeat the enemy ahead of time or invite God's speedy deliverance when faced with spiritual attacks. An effective spiritual tool to wade off spiritual attacks while advancing God's agenda upon the earth.

With over 1000 situation-specific prayers inspired by the Holy Spirit, Rapid Fire brings into your focus the major spiritual battles you need to confront to live your purpose with great ease. Rapid Fire Prayer focus areas include spiritual maturity, marital life, health, finances, destiny, deliverance from strongholds of foundations, strongholds of the mind, witchcraft powers, ancestral curses, and the spirit of untimely death. Rapid Fire will bring you to the forefront of your spiritual life to take the apostolic steps needed to fulfill your prophetic destiny and reduce your enemy to a footstool

DEDICATION

The book, **Rapid Fire**, is dedicated to the Person of the Holy Spirit who continues to indwell us and teaches us all things. Your presence has revealed to us the mysteries of heaven and Your fire of revival has lightened up all the former dark areas of our lives. Thank you Holy Spirit, Our Friend.

CONTENT

DELIVERANCE

RAPID FIRE PRINCIPLES OF UNDERSTANDING SPIRITUAL ATTACKS

1. Spiritual immaturity is an attack against the soul and the mind.
2. Spiritual attacks are launched against a marriage to block couples or children from advancing a purpose of God
3. Death attacks are launched to snatch a life prematurely and hinder God's assignment.
4. Witchcraft is a major tool used to launch spiritual attacks
5. A health attack is launched to get your body to fight against you.
6. Financial attacks are launched to tie you down to where you are not supposed to be and prevent you from fulfilling your God-given assignment
7. An attack of the mind and brain is launched to keep you from thinking right.
8. A destiny-derailing attack is launched to prevent you from fulfilling your destiny

The knowledge of the Lord Jesus and the mastery of the spiritual right tools can help you win. In this book, you will read literature, and prayer technical prayers, that speak to the devices and tactics of of enemy spiritual attack.

1

THE RAPID FIRE
PRAYERS

"For Let the high praises of God be in their mouth, And
a two-edged sword in their hand, To execute vengeance
on the nations, And punishments on the peoples;To
bind their kings with chains, And their nobles with
fetters of iron; To execute on them the written judgment
Psalm 149:6-9NKJV

Spiritual attacks are a different type of warfare,
launched by the enemy to attack, cripple,
distract from fulfilling a purpose. Spiritual
attacks are confused with all other types of
spiritual battles waged by the enemy.

When many are held captive or are on the
defense, the Lord commands that the children
of light forge ahead into the offensive line at

the forefront to defeat the enemy's battle plans against their life's calling and assignment. Rapid fire pushes you into apostolic acts and positions where the requirements of your life's calling are met and your prophetic destiny fulfilled.

Your assignment here on earth is an important one. It's very important to God that you fulfill your assignment, and also beneficial to you that you work according to the purpose you have been called.

Some questions for you?

1. Have you ever noticed, that when you are about to venture out to fulfill that important assignment, the enemy throws all forms of fiery darts, and one thing leads to the other, and then it never ends?

2. Have you sought spiritual growth, or ministry establishment and then met with all forms of perversion and oppression?

3. Have you been on the road to marriage, or in a marriage, then the enemy spins up a dirty battle?

4. What about finances? Has the enemy led you into one slippery slope to bury your head in debt or steal sources of livelihood from you?

5. On destiny, are you living outside of your destiny right now, or you are convinced that God planned a better plan for you and you're not living close to what is in stock for you?

The Rapid Fire Story

Rapid Fire, as the name implies describes God's speed deliverance at the battlefront. God had called us into ministry, and we were starting; One of the mandates we received was that **"He will raise a curseless generation"** through our ministry. As our ministry started, the Lord started His works of deliverance in people's foundation. This encounter was documented, and as we proceeded into the draft phase of the Uncursed book (a foundational Deliverance manual), major opposition began and serious spiritual battles arose. Those involved in the Uncursed project recorded swelling of hands, sudden wrist problems, and different types of attacks. The Lord said this type of work requires "Rapid-fire prayers. At this point, the Lord led us into heavenly methods of effective and apostolic prayers which opens the doors to one's life's calling. Rapid Fire book was birthed forth in the onset of God's move in the earlier days of our Prophetic and Apostolic ministry. It is a book powered by God's covenant of rapid activation of deliverance from evil attacks and prosperity in offensive battles. Since we first published Rapid Fire in 2018, God's work through Rapid Fire has been ongoing. Rapid Fire has become a prayer companion, read in different nations of the world; by all types of people; men, women, young and old, church leaders, ministers, and Christian professionals. Many people have shared their testimonies of God's move in their lives through their Rapid Fire encounters. We are thankful to all those who read the first version, and the updated version.

About Rapid Fire

Rapid Fire brings into focus prayers to launch against specific types of attacks or enemy attack potential. Rapid Fire prayers are biblical prayers. Some rapid-fire prayers attack the power of the enemy which seeks to hide behind a cultural veil. For example; witchcraft manifestations, and methods vary from location to location. In the Rapid Fire book, the fire of God is unleashed upon the power of witchcraft, in whatever ways it seeks to manifest or through whatever devices it seeks to use. Hence, you will find prayers targeted at different areas, methods, and devices of a particular type of power. All Rapid Fire prayers are biblical, and the Rapid Fire book should not replace your time in the Word of God.

Rapid Fire Chapters

Rapid Fire is divided into chapters. Each chapter represents a major area of spiritual warfare. In some of these chapters, prayers address sub-areas of spiritual warfare.

We have listed the major spiritual battles you need to address to function in your calling. Victory in these battles means you will sail smoothly in the ship of your life and fulfill your divine purpose with greater ease. Success in those areas will save you more time and ensure that your life does not end up as a waste. These battles include Spiritual maturity, Marriage, Health, Finances, Mind and Destiny. Deliverance from strongholds of foundations, strongholds of the mind, witchcraft, ancestral curses, and the spirit of untimely death should be actively pursued by any christian seeking to walk in freedom and make their lives count. Thankfully, military-like tactics and weapons are given to every Christian to win in spiritual warfare.

Rapid Fire Deliverance is a manual for deep deliverance and spiritual warfare, with situation-specific prayers inspired by the Holy Spirit. In the book, you will find prophetic prayers to destroy the altars of darkness, recover plundered glories, and heavily guard your life from spiritual harassment. When these prayers are used effectively, you will experience God's revival fire in your life. Do not be surprised if you find strange prayers to crack open ancient secrets, destiny-repairing prayers, prayers for divine healing, and prayers for troubled marriages as you read and pray. Rapid Fire has brought unheard-of testimonies into the lives of people. If you're oppressed or cast away, lost in life, the prayers in Rapid Fire will help you break free, as long as you have faith, stay free of sin, and live in obedience to God.

Rapid Fire is for you if...
1. You are a sinner and seeking restoration
2. Newly saved and searching for God's power
3. You have been lukewarm in your faith and want a radical change in your life

4. You face aggressive opposition in all life's endeavors

5. You are facing aggressive spiritual attacks

6. Your glory has been re-wired and you need a repair of destiny

7. You have lived your life communing with demons, psychics, mediums, and witches, and seeking the fresh fire of God to chase them out of your destiny

8. You are hungry for God and want to walk in God's supernatural power.

9. You want to live within the hedge of God's power.

10. You want to encounter Yahweh's power like the days of the Apostles.

11. You want to set up an anti-missile defense around your life to protect your life and destiny from evil attacks.

This may not be the book for you if...

You are unrepentant and living in sin as you would be open to more attacks from the enemy.

Using Rapid Fire Effectively

Repent from all sins

If there's any active sin in your life, repent today and say this prayer:

Father, I accept Jesus Christ as my Lord and Savior. I pray that you wash me clean with the Blood of Jesus. Forgive me of my sins in the name of Jesus, Forgive me the sins of my ancestors in the name of Jesus. Let the mercy of God speak for me. Let your grace speak for me and redeem my soul. Reveal the fullness of your glory to me, in the name of Jesus.

After you have said that prayer, do not return to sin.

A life of consecration

The more you yield your life to Jesus, the more spiritual authority you hold. Yielding your life to Jesus means you live your life in obedience to God's Word and the leading of the Holy spirit. God has so much love for you and wants you to walk in His ways. He does not compromise and will not create an exemption for you. He has set standards. His grace and love will help you fly high to reach those standards.

Deep Worship

Live a life of worship. Exalt the King of kings, the Lord of lords, the God of Abraham, Isaac and Jacob, the Holy One of Israel, Your Maker, the God who restores, the God who provides, the Great Physician, the Great I am! Exalt Him with songs, with praises, with thanksgiving, sing songs that glorify His name. Also, live a life that worships God.

Study the Word of God

Reading the Word of God is a fruitful spiritual exercise. Through it, you will be healed, delivered, restored, and receive a message from the Lord.

Journal

Write down dreams, visions, revelations, and ideas. In the revelations are wisdom, instructions, directions, deep secrets, and answers.

Fast and Prayers

A fasted and prayerful life are major tools in the arsenal of the believer who wants to advance into spiritual warfare. Some spiritual battles cannot be won without fasting and prayers. *"So He said to them, "This kind can come out by nothing but prayer and fasting" - Mark 9:29*

Vigils

Pick your time, make an appointment with God. You may begin at 11 PM or 12 midnight, and end at 3AM, 5 AM, or till as long as you are led by the Holy Spirit. Pick a chapter that applies to you, avoid all sorts of distractions read the Scriptures, make the confessions, and pray the prayers in the chapter.

JOURNAL

2

SPIRITUAL MATURITY

"For those who are led by the Spirit of God are the children of God"

Romans 8:14

There is no drought of the raw power of God, there is the shortage of willing vessels to carry His power. The Lord is constantly igniting pockets of His revival and He seeks the remnants who will carry His fire. We live in times where every believer must be filled with the power of the Holy Spirit to live an excellent life. Before you take off in life, you must be fully immersed in the Holy Spirit who will continually dispense insights and efficiencies to you. A Christian should never live in bondage or oppression of any form because of the power made available through the blood of Jesus. Unfortunately, the fake lion (enemy) scares God's children with false barking because Christians have not fully maximized the power in the blood of Jesus and prayers. That is why every Christian must be spiritually loaded up with the raw power of God. A spiritually powerful life begins with repentance, brokenness, and holiness. When you say hello to a lifestyle of holiness, you begin to live a life that puts Jesus first, a life that lives in awareness of the bloody cross of Jesus Christ, one led by the truth of the word of God and directed by the Holy Spirit. You look back at your sinful days and burst into tears, because you realize you were deserving of his wrath, yet God showed you His mercy and His kindness which brought you to repentance.

You set a new goal to meet God in heaven at the end of your earthly journey. Your new goal comes with a price - bidding farewell to worldly pleasures, chasing a higher calling, and living in full obedience to God. Your new spirit-filled lifestyle is like a downpayment to heaven. When you made that decision to acknowledge that Jesus died for you and accept that He is your Savior, you have chosen a path that leads to heaven. To follow through, you can't remain a baby in your faith, you need to pursue spiritual growth and development.

As a Christian, your quest for spiritual growth is not a one-time activity, it is a continuous journey which you must integrate into your everyday life.

WHAT IS SPIRITUAL MATURITY?

"But you shall receive power (ability, efficiency, and might) when the Holy Spirit has come upon you, and you shall be My witnesses in Jerusalem and all Judea and Samaria and to the

ends (the very bounds) of the earth."
Acts 1:8.

A believer is spiritually mature when they can take spiritual authority over spiritual situations through the power of the Holy Spirit. Spiritual maturity is accomplished through an ongoing relationship with the Lord. It is not a one-time endeavor. It is a process of continuous spiritual growth. It can be achieved only when the flesh is put to death and the Holy Spirit is allowed to take full control. When the Holy Spirit dwells in the life of a believer, He comes along as a Teacher, Helper, and Comforter and also takes diverse roles as needed or as the situation changes.

The Holy Spirit is God's active power within you. If you are praying for healing, the Holy Spirit can activate the healing anointing that has been dispensed upon you to make that healing manifest. He can grant you revelations as needed and also to give you solutions to problems. The world would be flooded with more inventions if Christian professionals carried the power of the Holy Spirit much more than they currently do.

Every believer has a role to play in their spiritual growth. Like education, after you are done with the fundamentals, you graduate from elementary to an intermediate spiritual level, and advance. In the spiritual realm, you never stop learning and growing.

"Therefore let us move beyond the elementary teachings about Christ and be taken forward to maturity, not laying again the foundation of repentance from acts that lead to death, and of faith in God"
Hebrews 6:1

This chapter ensures that you load up on prayers, and leads you into a lifestyle that sets you in motion for spiritual maturity. Without growth in the spirit, most of the problems afflicting Christians cannot be conquered. As you launch into the realm of spiritual maturity, your strongest foundation will be the word of God and the power of the Holy Spirit.

SOURCE OF SPIRITUAL POWER

There are highly organized demonic

governments and institutions, princes and princesses, queens and kings, powers and principalities, thrones and kingdoms, on the earth, underwater, in the air and the heavens.

"Wherein in time past ye walked according to the course of this world, according to the prince of the power of the air, the spirit that now worketh in the children of disobedience"
Ephesians 2:2

"For our struggle is not against flesh and blood, but against the rulers, against the authorities, against the powers of this dark world and against the spiritual forces of evil in the heavenly realms."
Ephesians 6:12

Those who practice witchcraft, sorcery, and magic arts obtain their powers and resources from the dark kingdom. Their major goal is to populate hell. They are the spiritual agencies that specialize in the destruction of destinies, the affliction of souls, the trading of souls, slavery, the destruction of marriages, and other wicked acts.

"This is what the Sovereign LORD says: What sorrow awaits you women who are ensnaring the souls of my people, young and old alike. You tie magic charms on their wrists and furnish

them with magic veils. Do you think you can trap others
without bringing destruction on yourselves?"
Ezekiel 13:18

JESUS, THE HEAD OF ALL POWERS

Thankfully, Jesus sits above and surpasses them all. He is the Commander of all governments, He carries all governments on His shoulders. He sits as the HEAD above all powers and has dominion over all hierarchies of darkness. As a Christian, you are connected to Jesus, as His son or daughter. You have His DNA within you and through His power, you can defeat all these lesser evil powers.

"and in Christ you have been brought to fullness. He
is the head over every power and authority" -
Colossians 2:1

The source of the ultimate spiritual power is the Lord Jesus Christ, who paid with His blood and died for our sins. The Lord freely gives His power to everyone who confesses that He is Lord and obeys His words.

"Behold, I give you the authority to trample on serpents and
scorpions, and over all the power of the enemy, and nothing

shall by any means hurt you"
Luke 10:19

Spiritual power is scarce because there are only remnants of believers who obey and genuinely worship.

REWARDS OF SPIRITUAL POWER

Ongoing Relationship with God

It is great to seek the Lord when you are looking for a solution, it is greater and more blessed to seek the Lord just to get to know Him. God is looking for people with this type of mindset.

"God is Spirit, and those who worship Him must worship in spirit and truth"
John 4:24

He is a rewarder of those who diligently seek Him. The truest and purest relationship you could ever have is with God. When you are in constant communion with your Manufacturer, your heart syncs with His, you know His will and live in obedience to it. He leads you right and takes care of all that concerns you.

Your level of relationship with the Lord impacts your level of spiritual awareness and authority. The person who is more spiritually aware understands the tones and the undertones of any environment but the person who is more spiritually powerful controls it. With your spiritual authority, you can command the day, intercede for friends and family, communities and nations, heal the sick, and break curses. You can decree that situations work according to God's design.

Living in the Spirit

The spirit of God is mandatory for heaven-seeking christians. With God's power upon your life, the Holy spirit is living and active in your life. Living in the spirit gives you the spiritually competitive edge because you are in tune with the heart of the Lord.

When you are faced with complex life choices, the spirit of God helps you discern, and gives you insights and solutions to problems. No longer will you say generic prayers, but the Lord will grant you customized prayers for speedier answers.

Engage and Win in Spiritual Warfare

Spiritual warfare means you strategically use spiritual weapons to fight in the spirit. You are not fighting with a physical group of people but against enemies who conduct their operations through demons, powers, and principalities in the spiritual realm.

Ignoring spiritual warfare has been a "safe haven" for many Christians. They take the dangerous route of "fleeing" and not officially adopting spiritual warfare as part of their regular christian lives. The deception of the enemy has led some believers to think they do not need to engage in spiritual warfare. The Bible clarifies that Jesus Christ and the Apostles did not ignore the demons but tactfully halted their operations in the lives of people.

"However, this kind goes not out but by prayer and fasting"
Matthew 17:21

"But if I with the finger of God cast out devils, no doubt the

kingdom of God is come upon you"
Luke 11:20

Every christian is part of ongoing spiritual warfare, and it is best to be *a good soldier of Jesus Christ* - 2 Timothy 2:3, and not the bad soldier who gets injured in the fight due to negligence. Remember, a good soldier doesn't ignore the attacks, a good soldier *fights the good fight* - 1 Timothy 6:12.

When you are loaded with the power of the Holy Spirit, you are fully equipped to overcome all that stands against you. The deeper you take your relationship with God, the stronger you become in spiritual warfare. You do not need to be a prophetic minister or pastor to live a victorious christian life. As a business owner, student, pilot, medical practitioner, or author, you also can dismantle the works of darkness, disband demonic groups, nullify wicked powers, and set perimeters of God's fire around your life. Before you can do all these, you need to grow up spiritually and continuously receive massive deposits of God's power in your life to engage successfully in spiritual warfare and live a prosperous christian life.

Trials will come to challenge your faith. Without spiritual warfare, there will be no miracles, and the devil's opposition will continue to arise. Until you are in a spiritual state where you can shut down covens of witchcraft, silence storms, disgrace demons, and expel them out of their hiding places, then can you advance spiritually.

A successful spiritual life requires a great depth of consecration and continuous times of waiting on the Lord. Without God's power, a person runs on empty and has no testimony to bear Jesus' witness. That is why Jesus told His disciples not to launch out until they receive the Holy Spirit:

"On one occasion, while he was eating with them, he gave them this command: "Do not leave Jerusalem, but wait for the gift my Father promised, which you have heard me speak about. For John baptized with water, but in a few days you will be baptized with the Holy Spirit."
Acts 1:4-5

Every believer must understand that there is no power without discipline. The power of God is released upon only disciplined and tested vessels.

THE PRICE OF SPIRITUAL GROWTH

1. Repent from all sins.
2. Accept Jesus Christ as your Lord and Savior.
3. Live a life of holiness.
4. Study and meditate on the word of God.
5. Fast and pray.

PRAYERS FOR
SPIRITUAL MATURITY

- Confess and repent from all your sins.
- Build a life and relationship with the Lord.

Worship

- Build a worship altar to the Lord
- Spend 12 minutes in worship before you say the prayers.

Personalize the following bible passages:

"but you will receive power when the Holy Spirit has come upon you; and you shall be My witnesses both in Jerusalem, and in all Judea and Samaria, and even to the remotest part of the earth."
Act 1:8

"And behold, I am sending forth the promise of My Father upon you; but you are to stay in the city until you are clothed with power from on high."
Luke 24:49

"Behold, I give unto you power to tread on serpents and scorpions, and over all the power of the enemy: and nothing shall by any means hurt you"
Luke 10:19

1. Lord, I thank you for your power and the provision of the Holy Spirit.

2. Every power that has cut me off from heaven's supply, is destroyed by the consuming fire of God in the name of Jesus.

3. Thou spirit of iniquity, be snuffed out of my foundation by the blood of Jesus.

4. Power of the Holy Ghost, overshadow my life in the name of Jesus.

5. Every legal foothold that I have given to the powers that stunt spiritual growth, let the blood of Jesus wipe it away in the name of Jesus.

6. My Father, clothe me with your garment of righteousness in the name of Jesus.

7. My Father, clothe me with your garment of holiness in the name of Jesus.

8. Every demonic spirit of lethargy that wants to put me to sleep when I'm

supposed to be spiritually awake, perishes in the name of Jesus.

9. Oh Lord of revelation, open my ears in the name of Jesus.

10. Let me hear what you are saying in every season of my life in the name of Jesus.

11. My Father, open my eyes, that I may see wondrous things of heaven, that I may see what you are doing in every season of my life in the name of Jesus.

12. My Father, open my eyes into the prophetic realm in the name of Jesus.

13. Let my spirit be tuned to heaven's broadcast in the name of Jesus.

14. Enroll my life in the school of your firepower in the name of Jesus.

15. Set me free from every ordinance of sin and iniquity in the name of Jesus.

16. Holy Ghost Fire, sanitize my life in the name of Jesus.

17. My Father - I surrender my senses(sight, smell, touch, taste & feeling) to you in the name of Jesus.

a. If you are interested in knowing how the Lord speaks, this is a prayer you can pray continuously till you begin to experience the Lord speak to you.

18. Take over my senses, my sense of sight, hearing, smell, taste, touch, knowing and use it for your glory in the name of Jesus.

19. Power of the Holy Ghost, infill me, infill my spirit in the name of Jesus.

20. O' Lord give me the power to become your faithful witness in the name of Jesus.

21. Let my life be a testimony of who you are, Lord Jesus.

22. Power of God, come upon my life in the name of Jesus.

23. The power of resurrection that makes a difference in the life of a believer comes into my life in the name of Jesus.

24. Holy Spirit, come upon me, in the name of Jesus.

25. My Father, Sanctify me for your use in the name of Jesus.

26. My spirit receives the strength of the Holy Spirit in the name of Jesus.

27. My father, clean me for your use in the name of Jesus.

28. Lord purify my stream in the name of Jesus.

29. I only want to hear from you Lord, not from the demonic realm in the name of Jesus.

30. Oh Lord, I receive accuracy of direction from You in the name of Jesus.

31. My father, amplify your communication signals in my life in the name of Jesus. (the way that the Lord speaks to you, it will no longer be vague, when He amplifies His communication signal in your life, you'll be able to hear clearly. You'll know how God speaks to you).

32. Every demonic cloud of darkness over my destiny, move away from me in the name of Jesus.

33. My father, help me not to defile my garment before you in the name of Jesus.

34. Help me O Lord to be able to meet your requirements of holiness in the name of Jesus.

35. My father, help me to heed your instructions before it is too late for me in the name of Jesus.

36. Every power that has undermined the greatness of God in my life, be disgraced and destroyed in the name of Jesus.

37. Every arrow targeted at my spiritual downfall, be destroyed in the name of Jesus.

38. Every destiny derailing spirits, the Lord destroys you in the name of Jesus.

39. Every power that wants to disgrace God in my life, your end has come, be exposed, be disgraced, and be destroyed in the name of Jesus.

40. Every arrow of lethargy in the place of prayer, O Lord disgrace them in the name of Jesus.

41. Powers seeking to turn my God into a liar, or into a lazy God, let the earth open up in the order of Korah, Dothan,

and Abiram consume those powers in the name of Jesus.

42. My life, you must count for eternity in the name of Jesus.

43. Power manipulating my dream life is destroyed in the name of Jesus.

44. The testimony of Jesus Christ is the spirit of prophecy, spirit of prophecy, fall upon me as I testify about Him in the name of Jesus.

45. Energize my inner man to always be ready for battle in the name of Jesus.

46. Lord Jesus, destroy every doubting and wandering spirit in my life in the name of Jesus.

47. Thou tireless enemy of my soul, your end has come, be utterly destroyed in the name of Jesus.

48. Every Nebuchadnezzar spirit that wants me to rebel against God, be destroyed in the name of Jesus.

49. Set my feet on high, set my feet upon mount Zion where there is deliverance and holiness, in the name of Jesus.

50. Every lust of the flesh, I come against you in the name of Jesus.

51. Every power of deceit, be nullified over my life in the name of Jesus.

52. Pride of the heart, you have no hold over my life in the name of Jesus.

53. My father, amplify your communication signals in my life in the name of Jesus. (the way that the Lord speaks to you, it will no longer be vague, when He amplifies His communication signal in your life, you'll be able to hear clearly. You'll know how God speaks to you).

54. My mind be delivered from the rottenness of perdition in the name of Jesus

55. Thou Samson errors, following my destiny around, lurking around me, be destroyed, in the name of Jesus.

56. Thou spirit of error, you have no hold over my life in the name of Jesus.

57. My Father, sanctify my lips O' God, that they may give you praise continually in the name of Jesus.

58. Father, my salvation will not become history, in the name of Jesus.

59. Holy Ghost, arise, set my life on fire for your glory in the name of Jesus.

60. Lord Jesus, pull me out of the dumpster of darkness in the name of Jesus.

61. Lord, deliver me from unending filthiness in the name of Jesus.

62. Today marks the end of my life in the dumpster in the name of Jesus.

63. Lord Jesus, let not the cup of thirst for Your presence will run dry.

64. Lord Jesus, connect my stream to your stream in the name of Jesus.

65. Lord Jesus, as Your soul lives, let me not run dry of revelation.

66. I am walking in the cleanliness of the Lord Jesus in the name of Jesus.

67. I am delivered from spiritual slavery in the name of Jesus.

68. Thou spirit of Hiel of bethel who rebuilt Jericho, attempting to rebuild every stronghold that the Lord has destroyed in my life, you are rendered

impotent and cursed forever in the name of Jesus.

JOURNAL

3

MARRIAGE

"For this reason a man will leave his father and mother and be united to his wife, and the two will become one flesh"
Matthew 19:5

The simple marriage arithmetic you need to master is this: **Marriage = Jesus Christ + The Church**

The summary of the equation is the permanent union established between Jesus Christ and the Church, to become and remain one body. When couples get married they become one flesh, their marriage becomes a replica of the marriage of Jesus Christ and the Church. The earthly marriage is designed to be a copy of the marriage between the Lord Jesus and the church. Hence, marriage is a spiritual experience. The Scripture instructs the husband:

"Husbands, love your wives, just as Christ loved the church and gave himself up for her"
Ephesians 5:25

And the wife is instructed:

Wives, submit yourselves to your own husbands as you do to the Lord"
Ephesians 5:22

These are the divine principles which the church was founded on. The Lord Jesus Christ loved the church that He gave up His life for the church, and the church must submit to the leadership of Jesus Christ.

ATTACKS ON MARRIAGES

Many marriages are under attack in various ways. Some couples continue to live in rejection and loneliness despite being married. Some spouses live in oppressive conditions as the enemy aggressively contends for their places in the family.

The devil attacks marriages and seeks to ridicule an institution of God, thwart His divine plan, and hinder His glory in the lives of people. This is the same as there are so many attacks on the church today; for the church to become powerless and an attempt to discredit God.

Marriage is the gateway to the establishment of the family unit. The devil knows this and seeks to corrupt the family which is the source of the society. If transgression abides within the family, it is easy to spread out in the community. When a family raises godly children, the outcome is leaders after God's heart. The enemy understands that the righteous cannot advance much once the foundation is faulty, hence launching attacks on the family. Attacks show up in ways like strife, anger, polygamy, lying, abuse, adultery, rejection, manipulation, degenerated sex life, competition, third-party control, and other forms.

If there's already a crack in your marriage, or you're about to be married, desire to be married, remember it is never too early or too late to tune up your prayers. Marriages are exposed to attacks mainly because of transgressions and carelessness.

COMMON CAUSES OF MARITAL ATTACKS

1. Premarital sex: Sex is established by God only for the married, not for engaged couples, or friends.
2. Past sexual sins with past sexual partners or adultery, opens the door to attacks in marriage.
3. Generational curse in a lineage often breeds attacks in marriage.
4. Soul Ties: These are emotional linkages to past sexual partners.

5. Deception: Deception, a major tool of the enemy is the hiding place of marital attacks. When deception is present, you do not demolish the stronghold of lies in your life, your marriage will suffer.

Thankfully the resurrection power of Jesus Christ is available to deliver marriages from bondages and attacks. Our God is a compassionate God, who straightens all crooked paths and will restore and protect your marriage.

Who Should Pray these Prayers

1. The unmarried who want to secure their future marital destiny.
2. The married who want to guard their marriage with the power of God.
3. The married whose marriage has been hijacked by the enemy.
4. Those who want to continually secure your marriage.

Who Should NOT Pray these Prayers?

1. If you are not rightfully married or are living in sin.

2. If the person you are with is not your husband or wife.

3. If you are praying these prayers to win the favor of somebody else's wife or husband against their marriage.

PRAYERS FOR MARITAL DELIVERANCE

Repent from all your sins. Confess your sins one by one as you remember them to God.

Worship

Whenever you set up an altar of worship, the Lord comes down. Spend 12 minutes in worship before you say the prayers.

Personalize and meditate on the following bible passages:

"Therefore, since we have these promises, dear friends, let us purify ourselves from everything that contaminates body and spirit, perfecting holiness out of reverence for God"
2 Corinthians 7:1

"If we confess our sins, he is faithful and just and will forgive us our sins and purify us from all unrighteousness"
1 John 1:9

" Then he said to me, "Prophesy to these bones and say to them, 'Dry bones, hear the word of the Lord! his is what the Sovereign Lord says to these bones: I will make breath enter you, and you will come to life. I will attach tendons to you and make flesh come upon you and cover you with skin; I will put breath in you, and you will come to life. Then you will know that I am the Lord"

Ezekiel 37:4-7

1. Thank God for the grace and blood of the Lord Jesus Christ over your life, spouse and marriage.

2. Every legal foothold that I have given to the powers of darkness over my marriage is destroyed by the rapid fire of the Lord in the name of Jesus.

3. Foundational troubles in my marriage are consumed by the rapid fire of God in the name of Jesus.

4. Lord, build up your altar of worship in my home by your rapid fire in the name of Jesus.

5. Locate my spouse with your honor in the name of Jesus.

6. The dry bone in my marriage, wake up and receive the breath of God in the name of Jesus.

7. All my past sins, plaquing my marriage, are canceled by the blood of Jesus and consumed by the rapid fire of God in the name of Jesus.

8. Lord Jesus, let your blood of Jesus break every marital curse and the rapid fire of the Lord consumes its effect in my life.

9. Demonic surveillance against my marital life is consumed by the rapid fire of God in the name of Jesus.

10. Thou rapid fire of God, expose every collection of evil friends in my circle in the name of Jesus.

11. The honey of my life shall no longer be sour, let the sweetness of God enter into it in the name of Jesus.

12. The honey of my life, stop attracting houseflies in the name of Jesus.

13. Rapid fire of the Lord shall cast out the spirit of deception upon my marriage, in the name of Jesus.

14. Light of God, shine into my marriage in the name of Jesus.

15. Joy of the Lord, dwell in my marriage in the name of Jesus.

16. With the rapid fire of God, I cast out every spirit of strife and contention in my marriage in the name of Jesus.

17. With the rapid fire of God, I cast out every spirit of division in my marriage in the name of Jesus.

18. The spirit of competition in my marriage is cast out by the rapid fire of God in the name of Jesus.

19. The thief of my joy is destroyed by the rapid fire of God, in the name of Jesus.

20. The spirit of mental infidelity at work in my marriage is cast out by the rapid fire of God in the name of Jesus.

21. The spirit of emotional infidelity at work in my marriage is cast out by the rapid fire of God in the name of Jesus.

22. The spirit of financial infidelity at work in my marriage is cast out by the rapid fire of God in the name of Jesus.

23. The spirit of marriage destruction is cast out by the rapid fire of God in the name of Jesus.

24. The self-destroying spirit at work in my marriage is cast out by the rapid fire of God in the name of Jesus.

25. Thou spirit that overturns communication between my spouse and I, is cast out by the rapid fire of God in the name of Jesus.

26. The curse that forbids happy marriage at work in my marriage, is cast out by the rapid fire of God in the name of Jesus.

27. Every curse that cuts short a marriage, you are nullified with the blood of Jesus.

28. Lord, deliver myself and spouse from every yoke of sexual perversion that renews evil covenant in the name of Jesus.

29. Agents of marital destruction, I withdraw my marriage and spouse from you in the name of Jesus.

30. I pull down every demonic imagination against my marriage in the name of Jesus.

31. The power of the bondwoman over my marriage is cast out by the rapid fire of God in the name of Jesus.

32. The spirit of Delilah is cast out by the rapid fire of God in the name of Jesus.

33. The spirit of Jezebel is cast out by the rapid fire of God in the name of Jesus.

34. The spirit of Athaliah is cast out by the rapid fire of God in the name of Jesus..

35. The blood of Jesus claims my marriage from the legal foothold of the demonic and restores unto me in the name of Jesus.

36. Evil generational patterns, set to manifest over my marriage, are cast out by the rapid fire of God in the name of Jesus.

37. Thou stealers of joy and love, your power is nullified over my marriage in the name of Jesus.

38. My marriage is blessed beyond a curse in the name of Jesus.

39. The spirit of jealousy is cast out by the rapid fire of God in the name of Jesus.

40.   Evil influences over my marriage are cast out by the rapid fire of God in the name of Jesus.

41. Lord Jesus, expose, nullify and destroy the power of evil influence over my marriage.

42. The voices of the evil third parties in my marriage permanently silenced the rapid fire of God in the name of Jesus.

43. The voices of the evil advisers in my marriage permanently silenced the rapid fire of God in the name of Jesus.

44. Demonic food that my spouse and I have ingested is purged out by the rapid fire of God in the name of Jesus.

45. The intruders are cast out of my marriage by the rapid fire of God in the name of Jesus.

46. The door into my marriage is secured by the rapid fire of God in the name of Jesus.

47. My Father, show me the secrets of the safety of my marriage in the name of Jesus.

48. Idols of my parent's house, hindering the glory of God over my marriage are consumed by the rapid fire of God in the name of Jesus.

49. Idols of my in-laws' house, hindering the glory of God over my marriage are consumed by the rapid fire of God in the name of Jesus.

50. Demonic strangers afflicting my marriage are cast out by the rapid fire of God in the name of Jesus.

51. Lord Jesus, let your hedge of divine fire, set a perimeter around my marriage in the name of Jesus.

52. The joy of the Lord flows into my marriage like a river.

53. The beauty of the Lord flows into my marriage in the name of Jesus.

54. My spouse, receive divine anointing to fulfill your God-given purpose in my life.

55. I receive divine anointing to fulfill my God's given purpose in the life of my spouse.

56. Spies of darkness, assigned to my marriage from the depths of darkness shall meet with the destroying and rapid fire of the Lord, in the name of Jesus.

57. Lord restore your presence in my marriage, in the name of Jesus

58. Thou spirit of Hiel of Bethel who rebuilt Jericho, attempting to rebuild every stronghold that the Lord has destroyed in my life, you are rendered impotent and cursed forever in the name of Jesus.

JOURNAL

4

DELIVERANCE FROM THE SPIRIT FROM THE SPIRIT OF UNTIMELY DEATH

"With a long life I will satisfy him And let him see My salvation."

Psalm 91:16

As a christian, you must be heaven-focused and ready for the second coming of Jesus Christ. Jesus Christ will come anytime without giving anyone advanced notice. It is going to be the greatest surprise ever. Until then, you must continue to live your life to glorify the Lord in all you do, until the Lord calls you home.

To fulfill the assigned number of your years on earth, you must continue to activate the higher authority of Jesus Christ to guard your life from the spirit of untimely death. The spirits of untimely death are evil spirits that take out people before their ripe age and divine purpose is completed.

THE SPIRIT OF DEATH

The spirit of untimely death seeks to cut short people's lives while their purpose is left unfulfilled. The first case of untimely death is that of Abel, when his brother, Cain murdered him. Since then, lives have been destroyed through abortions, gunshots, accidents, disasters, drugs, and sudden reasons. Regardless of what it is called, it is all engineered from the pit of darkness and must be stopped. The spirit of death is responsible for the destruction of promising destinies. It is a wasting spirit that specializes in killing people at major points in their lives. This spirit ensures that great singers never sing their songs, intelligent doctors-to-be never save a life, presidents die before they attain power, parents die young, and destinies are wasted.

As you pray and live right before God, the power of untimely death will have no hold over your life. You should also faithfully apply the following principles of the Bible.

PATHS TO LONG LIFE

The paths to long life are guidance provided in the bible for us to stay away from trouble, waywardness, and evil that cuts short the disobedient ones.

1. **Absolute Obedience to God's Word.** Obedience to God's Word is one of the keys to long life as the Scripture reveals. In God's Word are the instructions and lessons to lead into the path of life and avoid the snares of the enemy *"If you walk in My ways, keeping My statutes and*

commandments, as your father David walked, then I will prolong your days." 1 Kings 3:14

2. **Fear the Lord.** The fear of the Lord delivers from all sorts of other fears. Other types of fears lead to death, while the fear of the Lord attracts the covering of God's angels. *"The fear of the LORD prolongs life, But the years of the wicked will be shortened"* Proverbs 10:27

3. **Honor your parents in the Lord.** Submission to parents is one which brings the reward of long life. *"Honor your father and your mother, that your days may be prolonged in the land which the LORD your God gives you.* Exodus 20:12

4. **Stay away from ill-gotten profits.** *A leader who is a great oppressor lacks understanding, But he who hates unjust gain will prolong his days. Proverbs 28:16*

5. **Stay out of a lifestyle of gossip and deception.** *For, "The one who desires life, to love and see good days, must keep his tongue from evil and his lips from speaking deceit.* 1 Peter 3:10

PRAYERS FOR DELIVERANCE FROM THE SPIRIT OF DEATH

- Confess and repent from all your sins.
- Build a life and relationship with the Lord.

Worship

- Build a worship altar to the Lord
- Spend 12 minutes in worship before you say the prayers.

Personalize and meditate on the following scriptures:

"God is to us a God of deliverances; And to GOD the Lord belong escapes from death"
Psalm 68:20

"In the days of His flesh, He offered up both prayers and supplications with loud crying and tears to the One able to save Him from death, and He was heard because of His piety"
Hebrews 5:7

1. Thank God for the grace and blood of the Lord Jesus Christ

2. Every legal foothold that I have given to the spirit of death, let the blood of Jesus wipe it away in the name of Jesus.

3. Every graveyard worker that has accepted to work against my destiny, thunder of God, strike them in the name of Jesus.

4. I will not die but to bring the glory of the Lord in the land of the living.

5. Every angel of death assigned against me, my life is not your portion, go back to your sender in Jesus' name.

6. Every demonic assassin hired against me, locate your sender and unleash terror upon your sender in the name of Jesus.

7. Every demonic covenant destroying the lives of people and ruining health, thou demon behind this covenant, be destroyed by the fire of God in the name of Jesus.

8. Every aggressive battle in my blood line, raging against my life, be destroyed by the consuming fire of God in the name of Jesus.

9. Every demonic cloud of sulfur and destruction, move away by the fire of God in the name of Jesus.

10. Every household demon that currently has access into my life, the fire of God, consume them in the name of Jesus.

11. Negative air, you will not blow unto me in the name of Jesus.

12. Every power that wants to transfer foundational problems into my life, the Lord disgraces you in the name of Jesus.

13. Every demonic priest, chanting death and destruction into my blood, be destroyed by fire in the name of Jesus.

14. Every demonic gathering of demonic elders, blowing the flame of trouble and evil over my life, perish by the fire in the name of Jesus.

15. Every gate of untimely death opened upon me, the finger of God, shut you in the name of Jesus.

16. Any power that wants to summon me from my body, begin to summon yourself, and perish in the name of Jesus.

17. I destroy the power of untimely death and coffin over my life in the name of Jesus.

18. Every power calling my name from inside a coffin to invite me into a coffin, I will not die, but the sword of the Lord cuts you into pieces and you are permanently destroyed in the name of Jesus.

19. The horn of wickedness will not be stuck on me in the name of Jesus.

20. The garment of the grave is disgraced over my life in Jesus name.

21. (Mention your name) - my name is not in the register of the dead, therefore, come back to life in the name of Jesus.

22. In the name of Jesus, let every covenant with death over my life and family be annulled by fire.

23. Every agreement I have made or made on my behalf with the realm of the dead shall not stand in the name of Jesus.

24. Every gathering of the wicked, against the sanity of my existence, against the semanticity, preservation of my existence, scatter and be destroyed by the consuming fire of God in the name of Jesus.

25. Every demonic hand pointing itself against me, to demand for my blood, to demand for my life, be silenced forever by the blood of Jesus, in the name of Jesus.

26. Thou tireless enemy of my soul, your end has come, perish in the name of Jesus.

27. My portion is not the grave, I will not die but live to declare the works of the Lord.

28. The remnant of death in my body is consumed by the rapid-fire in the name of Jesus.

29. Deliver me with your outstretched arms, from every entrapment of death in the name of Jesus.

30. Lord Jesus, nullify the plaque of death from my family of origin.

31. Affliction shall never rise again because my prayers are sealed with the blood and fire of the Holy Ghost.

32. Thou spirit of Hiel of Bethel who rebuilt Jericho, attempting to rebuild every stronghold that the Lord has destroyed in my life, you are rendered impotent and cursed forever in the name of Jesus.

33. Thank you Jesus for answered prayers.

JOURNAL

5

PRAYERS AGAINST WITCHCRAFT POWERS & COVENS

"Then He said to me, "Son of man, dig into the wall"; and when I dug into the wall, there was a door.
And He said to me, "Go in, and see the wicked abominations which they are doing there." So I went in and saw, and there—every sort of creeping thing, abominable beasts, and all the idols of the house of Israel, portrayed all around on the walls. And there stood before them seventy men of the elders of the house of Israel, and in their midst stood Jaazaniah the son of Shaphan. Each man had a censer in his hand, and a thick cloud of incense went up. Then He said to me, "Son of man,

have you seen what the elders of the house of Israel do in the dark, every man in the room of his idols? For they say, 'The Lord does not see us, the Lord has forsaken the land." - Ezekiel 8:7

DEALING WITH WITCHCRAFT

Just like the times of old when Ezekiel was shown the vision concerning the activities of some elders in Israel, people still engage in witchcraft to mess up the life of susceptible victims. They are everywhere with wide coverage and highly connected!

The spirit of witchcraft is responsible for major troubles afflicting souls today. More than anytime in history, witchcraft is now being deployed in upgraded ways because their technology has improved. Witchcraft is responsible for sales of people's virtue, trading of souls, and all sorts of wickedness. They wear masks to penetrate people's weak defenses. Witchcraft has infiltrated the communities starting from the churches. You find so many powerless churches being harrassed by witchcraft and oppression.

There are different dimensions to witchcraft. If you consult mediums, demonic/false prophets, practice divination, spiritist, psychics, magicians, you are practicing witchcraft because you are tapping into the power they are drawing from. Between 2017 and 2022, there are a number of people walking into our Prophetic Worship encounters saying they are witches. When witchcraft is being exposed by the Lord to this extent, how much more those who have been afflicted by the powers of witchcraft.

WITCHCRAFT AND DECEPTION

"for the children of this world are in their generation wiser than the children of light"
Luke 6:8

Witchcraft has mastered deception. This spirit wears a mask and it operates heavily under deception and false humility. People who are not in the spirit are unable to catch them. The witchcraft spirit is an expert at pointing all evidence away from themselves. They have a wide variety of demonic deceptive practices such as taking up other people's persona spiritually, showing up as other people in and manipulating spiritually.

WHAT YOU MUST KNOW ABOUT WITCHCRAFT

- The spirit of witchcraft is merciless.
- Witches have a strong network where they can pass on their victims around for the purpose of anonymity.
- A witch could be in your network, or family without you discovering because they are very good at hiding their works.
- You can not launch an attack against witchcraft operations without the power of God, otherwise they would waste your life.
- You should not confront a witch physically, but with fiery prayers and the power of the Lord.
- Witchcraft spirits are wicked spirits that hate mercy and compassion. As a result, there is no compassion in the place of

warfare to witchcraft spirits.

- Witchcraft spirits seek to subtly lure people into disobedience so they lose access to God's presence.

- Witchcraft spirits may attempt to discredit revelations by the Holy Spirit in order not to be exposed.

Witchcraft is to be confronted only with the raw power of God. You do not negotiate with witchcraft, you do not confront them through idle talks. You cannot appease this spirit because it thrives in wickedness.

PRAYERS FOR DELIVERANCE FROM WITCHCRAFT POWERS

- Confess and repent from all your sins.
- Build a life and relationship with the Lord.

Worship

- Build a worship altar to the Lord
- Spend 12 minutes in worship before you say the prayers.

Personalize and meditate on the following scriptures:

1. Thank you for your power of revelation Father.
2. Every legal foothold that I have given to witchcraft powers, let the power in the blood of Jesus revoke it and wipe it away in the name of Jesus.

3. Lord Jesus, expose and disgrace all witchcraft operations in my network in the name of Jesus.

4. Lord Jesus, expose and disgrace all witchcraft activities against my life in the name of Jesus.

5. My father, take my name out of every demonic archive in the name of Jesus.

6. When the gynecology of the earth is going to be written, Lord Jesus, let my name be in the vine in the name of Jesus.

7. Lord Jesus, blot out my name from all forms of demonic database in the name of Jesus.

8. Lord Jesus, remove my name from every demonic family roll call.

9. All demonic ordinances that have written me fruitless are wiped off by the blood of Jesus in the name of Jesus.

10. Lord Jesus, deliver me from every ancient prophetic curse that I might have been a part of. (When Joshua and the children of Israel were many years later,

someone tried to rebuild, this is an example of a prophetic curse)

11. Lion of Judah, step into my situation and roar against all enemies in the name of Jesus.

12. I decree that the rapid fire of the Lord consumes the spirit of fear chasing me away from my breakthrough in the name of Jesus.

13. Powers coming to supervise bondages in my life through dreams or other means are consumed by the rapid fire of the Lord.

14. Powers that have taken my belongings presenting on the demonic altar on demonic altar to harm me is consumed by the rapid fire of the Lord in the name of Jesus

15. Lord Jesus, let the rapid fire of the Lord consume all carefully concealed manipulation of the enemy in my life and my network seeking to sow the seed of death in my life.

16. Lord Jesus, by Your Word, let the earth open up and swallow the manipulators and the powers of the manipulators in the name of Jesus.

17. Lord Jesus, let the rapid fire of the Lord consume the demonic pots of darkness representing me on demonic altars, in any demonic covens and nullify its effect in the name of Jesus.

18. The rod of the wicked shall not rest upon my portion in the name of Jesus.

19. Lord Jesus, let the power seeking to turn me into a scapegoat be consumed by the rapid fire of the Lord in the name of Jesus.

20. Lord Jesus, let the powers seeking to cause an irrecoverable error in my life be destroyed by the rapid fire of Yahweh in the name of Jesus.

21. Lord Jesus, consume the powers of divination against my life by the rapid fire of Jesus.

22. Every power that has not gotten the memo that Jesus is Lord in my life, today

marks your end, perish in the name of Jesus.

23.Every fainting spell against me, perish by the consuming fire in the name of Jesus

24.Victory of Yahweh be my reality

25.Fire of the Holy Ghost, guide my mind against every manipulation and bewitchment, and insanity in the name of Jesus

26. Fire of the Holy Ghost, guide my mind against every demonic intrusion in the name of Jesus

27. Every demonic dedication upon my life, with your mighty right hand, Lord deliver and save me in the name of Jesus.

28.Every demonic attack against your star, be quenched by the fire of God in the name of Jesus.

29.My star is restored in the name of Jesus, my destiny is secured in Jesus

30. Every transatlantic demonic operation, forming a demonic strategic alliance against me and my family, fire of

God, burn them to ashes in the name of Jesus.

31. Every demonic spirit of lethargy that wants to put me to sleep when I'm supposed to be spiritually awake, perishes in the name of Jesus.

32. Every demonic hand placed upon my destiny, upon my belly, upon my eyes, upon my head, be cut off by the blazing sword of the Lord.

33. Every manifestation of witchcraft hand, against my destiny, Oh earth, swallow them up in the name of Jesus.

34. Every demonic hand, every witchcraft hand, against my life, manipulating my destiny, wither away in the name of Jesus

35. Every strange woman, owner of a strange hand, in the name of Jesus, perish by the fire of Jesus.

36. Every demonic gathering of the enemy against my life, against my destiny, perish in the name of Jesus.

37. Every demonic gathering of the enemy against my life, against my destiny, perish in the name of Jesus.

38. Every demonic collection of my hair against my destiny, be released in the name of Jesus.

39. Every demonic calabash bearing my name in demonic coven, in demonic altars, in demonic boxes, by the power in the of Jesus, shatter in the name of Jesus.

40. Lord, uproot everything that's not of you in my life in the name of Jesus.

41. My blood rejects bewitchment in the name of Jesus.

42. My soul, my body, spirit you are delivered from the snare of the flower

43. My father, deliver me from the coven and demonic gathering of witchcraft in Jesus name.

44. My soul, my body, spirit you are delivered from the snare of the fowler.

45. My father, deliver my virtues from the coven of witchcraft.

46. Every demonic representation of my destiny in demonic covens, be destroyed in the name of Jesus.

47. Every demonic monitoring network against my advancement, your time is up, perish in the name of Jesus.

48. Every power that has donated my name for evil, thunder of the Lord, locate them, shatter them and restore my destiny in Jesus name

49. Every coven that has my name in their demonic database, my life is not your candidate, lose me and let me go in the name of Jesus.

50. Every of my virtues, hidden in demonic crevices, let the fire of the Holy Ghost, retrieve them for me and locate me right now.

51. Every of my virtues hidden under active volcanoes, fire of the Holy Ghost, retrieve them for me.

52. Any power that wants to trade my life as derivative of trading my parents' life, perish by fire in the name of Jesus.

53. Every enchantment made against my name and destiny, let the voice of the Lord silence it in the name of Jesus.

54. Every enemy that has donated my destiny for a demonic cause, finger of God, retrieve my destiny, fire of God, burn them to ashes in Jesus name.

55. Every record bearing my name in a demonic warehouse, catch fire in the name of Jesus.

56. Every foreign lips and strange tongue against my life receive fire and be destroyed in the name of Jesus.

57. The God of my breakthrough, arise and breakthrough the enemies of my life like a damn in the name of Jesus.

58. My life and destiny shall not bow to witchcraft in the name of Jesus.

59. Lord, set me free from every demonic entanglement in Jesus name.

60. Every item representing my life in a demonic coven, let the thunder of the Lord, shatter them in the name of Jesus.

61. Every demonic thief fantasizing on crushing my dream, swallow yourself and perish in the name of Jesus.

62. Every demonic connection in my life that has gone unnoticed for so long, be exposed and destroyed in the name of Jesus.

63. Lord Jesus, let your rapid fire break open my destiny hidden in demonic prisons in the name of Jesus.

64. Every demonic sexual predator corrupting my destiny, be destroyed in the name of Jesus.

65. Every power that has received witchcraft to fight me, be consumed by Yahweh's fire in the name of Jesus.

66. Thou rod of the wicked, resting upon my life and family , be burned to ashes by the fire of the Holy Spirit.

67. Every demonic mantle transfer, my life is not available, the blood of Jesus covers my life in the name of Jesus

68. Lord, disgrace the power of the oppressor over my destiny in the name of Jesus.

69. Every witchcraft activity, lined up for my life, be consumed by the fire of the Holy Ghost in the name of Jesus.

70. Every demonic weight pulling me down, be cut off in the name of Jesus.

71. Every xray of darkness against my destiny, against my health, perish in the name of Jesus

72. Every demonic gang-up against the manifestation of my destiny, be shattered by fire in the name of Jesus.

73. Thou spirit of Hiel, attempting to rebuild all the strongholds of witchcrafts that the Lord has destroyed in my life, you are rendered impotent and cursed forever in the name of Jesus

74. Afflictions shall rise no more because I seal my prayers with the blood of Jesus and the fire of the Holy Spirit.

75. Glory and honor be to you Lord Jesus for answered prayers.

JOURNAL

6

BREAKING THE YOKE OF CURSES AND ANCESTRAL SINS

WHAT IS A CURSE?

Whenever a curse is in operation in the life of a person, it is there because it has been given a warrant, a right-of-stay, a permit to live freely, called a legal foothold. The legal foothold is granted by the Lord when an argument is won against a person in the court of heaven.

Curses are potent evil words, declared against the lives of people for punishment and to cause harm. Curses come by as a result of disobedience to God.

NOTABLE CURSES MENTIONED IN THE BIBLE

Confusion, no set direction, getting lost in life, wandering around, without insights or direction, abuse, and lack of help. Loss to enemies , oppression, robbery, inability to succeed, enemy attack, profitless labor, failure, poverty, scarcity of helpers, non-achievement

Curses also manifest in families and marriage situations: Anger, jealousy, unresolved conflicts, extra-marital affairs. fruits of the womb. Rape, Loss from hard labour, fruitlessness, loss of children, divorce, fornication, incest, adultery

Infirmities : Fever, cancer, rashes, boil, blindness, incurable diseases, tumors, madness, confusion of the mind. (Deuteronomy 28 :17-38).

A CURSE IN ACTION

How do you know that a person is under a curse? The Bible spells out what the appearance of curses look like. Curses manifest in various ways. Here's an example.

Take for instance the case of a young lady who is smart in school, gets distinctions, receives awards and heads to college. While in college, she loses focus, drops out, goes on to another school to re-enroll and continues to drop out of college. She manages to receive an Associate degree. While at the 7th college, she ran into trouble, unable to meet her course requirements, and had to change her college major to Accounting. While in Accounting, she failed her core requirements. She heads on to the next available department. She looked back into her family and found the pattern, none of her siblings successfully obtained a Bachelor's degree. She was determined to be free from the curse that had plagued her family line. Talk about the curses of confusion, no set direction, getting lost in life, wandering around, without insights or direction, inability to succeed, non-achievement and failure mentioned in Deuteronomy 28 at full display.

She begins serious curse- breaking prayers, with the mindset, " if this is the last thing I do, then it will be the first thing i'll tackle". Until then was she able to complete her Bachelor's degree. In total, she waited 11 years, attended 7 colleges, and passed through 5 majors before she got 1 bachelor's degree.

Watch out for the following symptoms in your own life, they might be as a result of a curse.

ROOTS OF CURSES

Curses can be handed over to several generations and keep people under subjection. It is clearly stated in the scripture that God visits the sin of parents upon the children up to the third and fourth generation.

"Now as Jesus was passing by, He saw a man blind from birth, and His disciples asked Him, "Rabbi, who sinned, this man or his parents, that he was born blind?" - John 9:1-3

Your sins could bring a curse upon you. Sins committed way before you were born could be the reason why you are placed under curses. The iniquity of your parents, grandparents, great grandparents could be the culprit.

BREAKING FREE FROM CURSES

Curses are not to be taken with levity. You need a mindset of determination to break free from curses. Breaking free from curses requires desperation and spiritual violence. Isaac told Esau, *"You will live by the sword and you will serve your brother. But when you grow restless, you will throw his yoke from off your neck"* Genesis 27:40.

Thankfully we have a High Priest who is full of mercy and whose blood was slain to wash our garments clean. His blood is powerful, and strong enough to break every curse.

"Blotting out the handwriting of ordinances that was against us, which was contrary to us, and took it out of the way, nailing it to his cross" - Colossians 2:17

Prayers to break free from curses should be prayed regularly and violently.

PRAYERS TO BREAK FREE FROM CURSES

Repent from all your sins. Confess your sins one by one as you remember them to God.

Worship

Whenever you set up an altar of worship, the Lord comes down. Spend 12 minutes in worship before you say the prayers.

Personalize and meditate on the following scriptures:

1. Every curse placed upon me, upon my destiny, upon my life, upon my reproductive organs, break by the power in the name of Jesus.

2. Every curse of thou shall not prosper working against my destiny break in the name of Jesus.

3. The demonic power and curse that seizes glory and borrows glory that the owner

of the glory never enjoys their glory, my head rejects you, perish by fire in the name of Jesus.

4. Every curse from glory to doom, curse from glory to failure that has plagued my ancestors, that has plagued my family line, that wants to make my life its next victim, I am not your victim, be broken by fire in the name of Jesus.

5. In the name of Jesus, every curse that entered into my life from the backyard, by the power in the name of Jesus be disgraced and leave in the name of Jesus.

6. Every curse of slow progress, break in the name of Jesus.

7. Every curse of no progress, break in the name of Jesus.

8. Every terror and curse associated with the lands that I have passed through, be nullified the name of Jesus.

9. Every ancestral power that wants to turn my blessings to sorrow to conform to their demonic heritage, be destroyed by the consuming fire in the name of Jesus.

10. The yoke of the unmarried bride, that breaks marriage, is broken upon my life in the name of Jesus.

11. Demonic custodian of foundational curses, be destroyed in the name of Jesus.

12. The curse of the sideway victory, be broken in the name of Jesus.

13. Lord, set me free from every demonic entanglement in Jesus name.

14. Demonic custodian of foundational curses, perish in the name of Jesus

15. Lord, purify my life with your power, in the name of Jesus.

16. Every curse of desolation against my destiny, be broken by the blood of Jesus.

17. Curses hiding to fight me, blood of Jesus, expose and destroy them in the name of Jesus.

18. I break the yoke of every aggressive enemy over my life in Jesus name.

19. Every aggressive battle in my blood line, raging against my destiny, perish by fire in the name of Jesus.

20. Battle that has been present in the foundation and attached to my life, be exposed, disgraced and destroyed in Jesus name.

21. Every manifestation of the orphan spirit in my destiny, be destroyed in the name of Jesus.

22. Every battle of the wrong identity that has been fighting my destiny, my life, be broken completely by the blood of Jesus.

23. Demonic elders decreeing curses against me, the thunder of God strikes you dead in the name of Jesus.

24. The yoke of the oppressor has been broken and I am delivered and set free in the name of Jesus.

25. Every viral warfare that entered into my life through my mouth by food, be nullified in the name of Jesus.

26. Every viral warfare that is attacking me because of my blood relations, be nullified in the name of Jesus

27. Thou spirit of Hiel, attempting to rebuild all the strongholds of ancient curses in

my life, you are rendered impotent and cursed forever in the name of Jesus

28. Afflictions shall rise no more because I seal my prayers with the blood of Jesus and the fire of the Holy Spirit.

29. Glory and honor be to you Lord Jesus for answered prayers.

JOURNAL

7

HEALTH

He said, "If you listen carefully to the LORD your God and do
what is right in his eyes, if you pay attention to his commands
and keep all his decrees, I will not bring on you any of the
diseases I brought on the Egyptians, for I am the LORD, who
heals you."
Exodus 15:26

Health problems may be spiritual or physical, but we will focus on the spiritual. The Lord commands us to obey and has laid down conditions attached to obedience. Curses brought about by sin are one of the leading causes of infirmities.

"There is no soundness in my flesh because of Your indignation; There is no health in my bones because of my sin".
Psalm 38:3

CAUSES OF INFIRMITIES

The Lord gave the consequences of disobedience in the book of Deuteronomy. (*Deuteronomy 28:20-28*)

1. **Confusion**: *The Lord will send on you curses, confusion and rebuke in everything you put your hand to, until you are destroyed and come to sudden ruin because of the evil you have done in forsaking him.*

2. **Diseases**: *The Lord will plague you with diseases until he has destroyed you from the land you are entering to possess.*

3. **Wasting diseases**: *The Lord will strike you with wasting disease, with fever and inflammation, with scorching heat and drought, with blight and mildew, which will plague you until you perish.*

4. **Tumors, sores, boils, itches, incurable**

diseases: *The Lord will afflict you with the boils of Egypt and with tumors, festering sores and the itch, from which you cannot be cured.*

5. **Blindness, confusion of the mind, madness:** *The Lord will afflict you with madness, blindness and confusion of mind.*

JESUS, THE GREAT PHYSICIAN

The healing power of the Lord is still very much around. He is the Lord that heals. His mercy is unlimited and he shows unto as many as will come humbly to seek his face.

Here are some healing examples from the bible;

1. He healed the woman who bled for 12 years who touched his clothes because of her faith *Matthew 9:20-22*
2. He healed the Blind Man at Siloam Pool *John 9:6-7*
3. Jesus went to towns and villages and healed every kind of diseases *Matthew*

9:35

4. Jesus healed the crippled man *Mark 2:9-12(a)*

As the days of old, we continue to experience the healing power of the Lord Jesus up till today.

TESTIMONIES OF HEALING

Revived From Coma

I received a text message from a Nigeria saying;

"My son is sick. He is an undergraduate in canada. He fell and sustained some head injury which they said affected his brain. I told them I don't believe their report. He has been on hospital admission since Sunday.Please join us in prayers for a miraculous healing process. We want to testify concerning this matter".

I called him immediately but he was unreachable by phone. I sent him a prayer voice message. During the week, he called back and we prayed again. the Lord showed a vision and I released the word. I saw the cross section of a brain, looks like two separate portions of the brain were disconnected. Then I saw something that looked like jellyfish on one side of the brain. The jellyfish began to swim across the other lifeless portion of the brain. This formed a link to the two brain lobes and they were able to function like one complete unit. This meant the Lord was bringing healing to his brain.

After about two weeks, he shared the following testimony:

"To God be the glory, my son is recuperating faster than expected. He has started walking and talking well. However the doctors insist that he must go to a rehab facility for sometime."

Hallelujah! Only the Lord can do this.

Signs of Colorectal Cancer Disappeared

In 2017, a sister called us for prayers. She had gone to the doctor 2 times and they discovered blood in her colon. Her doctor told her it might be a sign of colorectal cancer and a colonoscopy was scheduled. The night before her appointment, we spoke to her. As we began to pray, I heard the Lord say, don't pray, worship me. " We worshiped for about 8 minutes, then I heard the Lord say again, "tell her to rejoice". The next day she called to testify that there was no longer any sign of blood found in her colon. Glory to God.

Revived from Coma

A brother's organs were shutting down. He was on life support and the heart and other vital organs were deteriorating fast. His sister sent messages to request for prayers, she ended the text with "my brother is a perfect candidate for a miracle". I said to my wife, that is true, this is an opportunity for God to show His glory. As we prayed, the Lord showed me two machine-like objects between two organs.

The sister said those were the two defibrillators attached to his heart which was causing infections. The doctors also found drugs in his system which affected major organs. The family was told to get ready for end of life care.

The Lord said to me, "*I need someone who has authority in this life to contend for his life through prayers in my presence*". I asked the sister, "is your brother married", she said no. The next few days, we called to check back on the status of the man. He was still the same. I shared the revelation with the sister, The Lord said , "*I need someone who has authority in this life to contend for his life through prayers in my presence*". She said, that is true. His son has been saying he just wants his father to go and not suffer anymore. We prayed that the son (*the authorized person*) would have a change of heart and pray to God that his father's life be saved. After prayers, the sister texted us that there was a complete turn around, that his brother woke up from a coma and had been requesting food. This was the hands of God.

Although, this person eventually passed on after a few months afterwards due to the massive damage the drugs had done to his organs. Our hope is that he was able to meet with the Lord while he had a second chance.

KEEPING YOUR DELIVERANCE

Demons have the practice of re-visiting their old places. Not just that, they invite a host of other demons to come with them when they come along. If they find the place empty, they return with greater afflictions

"When an unclean spirit goes out of a man, he goes through dry places, seeking rest, and finds none. Then he says, 'I will return to my house from which I came.' And when he comes, he finds it empty, swept, and put in order. Then he goes and takes with him seven other spirits more wicked than himself, and they enter and dwell there; and the last state of that man is worse than the first. So shall it also be with this wicked generation."
Matthew 12:43-45

That's why christians are encouraged not to backslide, but seek the Lord more even after deliverance. To keep your deliverance, stay out of trouble, and do not return to your former sins. Do not be a God-user, who seeks for just the next miracle and goes back into their vomit. Hold on to holiness and keep building on your relationship with God.

"Afterward Jesus found him in the temple and said to him, See, you are well! Sin no more, that nothing worse may happen to you" - John 5:14.

PRAYERS FOR DELIVERANCE OF HEALTH

- Confess and repent from all your sins.
- Build a life and relationship with the Lord.

Worship
- Build a worship altar to the Lord
- Spend 12 minutes in worship before you say the prayers.

Personalize and meditate on the following scriptures:

1. Lord, surround me with your hedge of fire.

2. Evil arrow in my body, health, jump out and go back to your senders in the name of Jesus.

3. Any power feeding me food of affliction in my dream, feed them Lord with their own evil meal and nullify the effects of eating such evil food in my life, in the name of Jesus.

4. Every demonic power that is shedding its own blood to evoke pity from higher powers against my destiny, be destroyed and let the blood of Jesus speak for me in the name of Jesus .

5. My life, hear the Word, by the resurrection power of Jesus, arise from the position of death, be resurrected to life in the name of Jesus.

6. Spirit of cancer, I curse you to your roots, be melted by the fire of the Holy Ghost, in the name of Jesus.

7. Spirit of infirmity, get out of my life in the name of Jesus.

8. Every demonic operation of the enemy to harvest my sight, be destroyed by the

consuming fire of God in the name of Jesus.

9. Every seed in my body system attracting death, be destroyed by the fire in the name of Jesus.

10. Every monitoring device, tracking device, microphone device, monitoring my life and destiny for evil, let the thunder of the Holy Ghost destroy in the name of Jesus.

11. Every demonic intrusion into my body system, get out by the fire of God in the name of Jesus.

12. Every demonically inspired involuntary twitching of nerves cells in my brain, perish in the name of Jesus.

13. Every sickness of the destroyer, every form of cancer in my brain, perish by the fire of God, in the name of Jesus.

14. Veins in my brain, you will not rupture, in the name of Jesus.

15. Heavenly physician, visit every neuron in my brain, visit every section in my brain, in the name of Jesus.

16. Heavenly physician, visit all parts of my brain,

17. Lord, visit the foundation of my brain in the name of Jesus.

18. My father, every demonic seed deposited through my mouth into my system, be uprooted by fire, locate your sender for destruction, in the name of Jesus.

19. Every seed of hernia in my body, perish by fire in the name of Jesus.

20. Every seed of disease in my blood evaporates by the fire of God in the name of Jesus.

21. My Lungs, be healed in the name of Jesus.

22. My Diaphragm, be healed in the name of Jesus.

23. I come against every breathing sickness, the fire of God burns you to ashes in the name of Jesus.

24. Every irregular blood flow receives divine regulation by the power of God in the name of Jesus.

25. Demon of demonic odor and stench, get out of my life in the name of Jesus.

26.   Every disjointed knees be healed in the name of Jesus. Healing of the Lord, enter my knees.

27. Every ankle problem, be healed in the name of Jesus.

28. Every demonic tower of deception in my foundation, that has vowed to keep me in a dungeon of sickness, collapse and perish in the name of Jesus.

29. I break the yoke of every aggressive enemy of my health in the name of Jesus

30.   Cancer is not my portion.

31. Curable or incurable disease is not my portion.

32. Every arrow of paralysis fired into my body, go back to your senders in the name of Jesus.

33. I will not become lame or paralyzed in the name of Jesus.

34. My blood, reject bewitchment in the name of Jesus.

35. My father, any representation of my blood, taken into a demonic coven, let the coven be shattered and my blood be restored by the power in the blood of Jesus.

36. Every of my blood that is being used against my life, against my destiny, by the blood of Jesus, be nullified in the name of Jesus.

37. Every demonic pronouncement into the origin of my blood to harm me, be nullified by the blood of Jesus.

38. Every power appearing in the spirit realm by the virtue of my blood as me, to ruin my life, to ruin my destiny, your end has come, perish in the name of Jesus.

39. Because the blood of Jesus flows through me, my blood cannot be manipulated.

40. Every demonic priest, chanting death, destruction into my blood, be destroyed by the thunder of God in the name of Jesus.

41. My blood line receives the infusion of the blood of Jesus, in the name of Jesus.

42. My father, by the covenant that established the moon, the sun and star, cursed be anyone or any spirit or any power that curses my blood in Jesus name.

43. I plug my life into heaven's power source, in the name of Jesus.

44. Blood of Jesus, while I am still living, speak for me in the name of Jesus.

45. Insanity is not my portion in the name of Jesus.

46. Every demonic poison in my body, your time is up, be uprooted by fire of the Holy Ghost, and be offloaded upon your sender in the name of Jesus.

47. Every demonic food, I have ingested, fire of God, purge them out in the name of Jesus.

48. The yoke of mental imbalance broken in the name of Jesus.

49. Every disease of the bones that the enemy is using to fight me, to fight my

future, let those infirmities of the bones return to their sender.

50.   I will not be cut short in the name of Jesus.

51. My life will not be lived in sickness in the name of Jesus.

52. I come against every demonic poison, fired into my system, locate your sender for destruction.

53. The peace of the Lord reigns upon my life in the name of Jesus.

54.   Every flesh eating power employed against my destiny eat your own flesh and drink your own blood like sweet wine in the name of Jesus.

55. Every power hired against me, employed to eat my flesh and drink my blood, by the power in the name of Jesus, eat your own flesh and drink your own flesh like sweet wine in the name of Jesus.

56. I receive the life of God in the name of Jesus.

57. Blockage in my heart, be flushed out by the blood of Jesus.

58. My heart, function as you have been created in the name of Jesus

59. Thou spirit of Hiel, attempting to rebuild all the strongholds of infirmity in my life, you are rendered impotent and cursed forever in the name of Jesus

60.   Afflictions shall rise no more because I seal my prayers with the blood of Jesus and the fire of the Holy Spirit.

61. Glory and honor be to you Lord Jesus for answered prayers.

JOURNAL

8

FINANCES

Instead, make your top priority God's kingdom and his way of life, and all these things will be given to you as well.
Matthew 6:33

Those who have mastered the principles of finances are those who understand the principles of inheritance. They know that God is the Commander-in-Chief of all resources.

"The earth is the LORD's, and everything in it, the world, and all who live in it"
Psalm 24:1

You also need to remember we are not called to a lifestyle of money-chasing, but we are called to worship.. When you love the Lord so much that you worship Him and set your priority towards heaven, He releases heaven's resources to you. It becomes a Father-son and Father-daughter affair, where the enemy cannot place a limit on the use of father's resources.

FINANCIAL ATTACKS EXPLAINED

The spirit of mammon strikes by taking the place of God in the hearts of people. It lures people to seek after earthly treasures and deviates from a life of worship.

It also goes into the people's finances to find a void. Once there is a void, it goes in to eat up and expand the void beyond control. A person can invite the spirit of mammon into their finances when they get into debt. Certain ideologies are set in place by the enemy to defraud people of their inheritance. The enemy tricks people out of inheritance and keep them in slavery through a lifestyle of debts. *"The rich rule over the poor, and the borrower is slave to the lender". Proverbs 22:7.*

Whatever you do, do not get into debt, if you are already in debt, jump out of it. The only way you can jump out of it is to pray for financial deliverance. He is merciful and will give you ideas and resources to jump out of debt and you will be set free.

How do you really tell if you are under financial attack? The Holy Spirit will teach you all things and can help you diagnose that. Refer back to chapter 1 of this book to learn how you can pray your way through to receive the power of the Holy Ghost.

Remember, like any other kind of attacks, the first step is to identify what the problem is with the help of the Holy Spirit, before you can get it resolved.

Financial attacks continue to manifest in various ways. Let's take a look at the major causes of financial attacks.

MAJOR CAUSE OF FINANCIAL ATTACK

Curses manifests as debt, toil without rewards, waste and failure.

You will sow much seed in the field but you will harvest little, because locusts will devour it. You will plant vineyards and cultivate them but you will not drink the wine or gather the grapes, because worms will eat them. You will have olive trees throughout your country but you will not use the oil, because the olives will drop off.
You will have sons and daughters but you will not keep them, because they will go into captivity. Swarms of locusts will take over all your trees and the crops of your land. The foreigners who reside among you will rise above you higher and higher, but you will sink lower and lower. They will lend to you, but you will not lend to them. They will be the head, but you will be the tail."
Deuteronomy 28: 38-44

Under these curses, no matter how hard a person works, the result is fruitlessness, waste and no reward. Even if a reward comes, it ends in ruin. Those under this curse are unable to do anything tangible with earnings and savings before it disappears. This curse is responsible for profitless hard work, waste, toiling without rewards, self-destructive habits, Debt, bankruptcy, working hard without savings, loss of employment, failure in business.

These curses also push us to form destructive habits like amassing debts, living flamboyantly, spending unreasonably, mismanaging funds, and making all sorts of foolish decisions with money.

OTHER CAUSES OF FINANCIAL DISTRESS

Some financial hardships are not due to curse or spiritual attacks. They show up in people's lives because they were invited.

Mismanagement and Lack of Planning

A popular saying goes, "if you fail to plan, you plan to fail. Mismanagement and lack of financial planning is likely to end in financial ruin. Spending on impulse without a plan or outside of budget are gateways to financial troubles.

"Suppose one of you wants to build a tower. Won't you first sit down and estimate the cost to see if you have enough money to complete it?

Luke 14:28

Flamboyant Lifestyles

A flamboyant lifestyle, a life devoid of simplicity will end in financial distress. When you live above your earnings, you are set up for failure.

"Those who love pleasure become poor; those who love wine and luxury will never be rich".
Proverbs 21:17

BREAKING FREE FROM FINANCIAL DISTRESS

Some financial distress could be resolved by isolating the root causes and fixing it by following these two rules;

1. Better management
2. Lifestyle changes

If your finances are under spiritual attacks, you need to get into spiritual warfare and pray that God delivers you.

BREAKING FREE FROM FINANCIAL ATTACK

1. The first thing you need to do is to repent before the Lord
2. Read and meditate on the bible
3. Pray the following prayer points for 21 days, starting at 12 midnight to 1AM each night or until you get a release in your spirit.
4. Give to causes sponsoring God's work on earth tithes and give offerings to the Lord. Although tithing is not mandatory in the bible, tithers have recorded positive results and are beneficiaries of promises of blessings attached to tithing.

The Bible specifically attached conditions to tithing:

"Bring the whole tithe into the storehouse, that there may be food in my house. Test me in this," says the Lord Almighty, "and see if I will not throw open the floodgates of heaven and pour out so much blessing that there will not be room enough to store it. I will prevent pests from devouring your crops, and

*the vines in your fields will not drop their fruit before it is
ripe," says the Lord Almighty"*
Malachi 3:10-11

PRAYERS AGAINST FINANCIAL DISTRESS

- Confess and repent from all your sins.
- Build a life and relationship with the Lord.

Worship

- Build a worship altar to the Lord

Spend 12 minutes in worship before you say the prayers.

Personalize and Meditate on the Following Scriptures:

1. Lord, I thank you for the power in the blood of Jesus.
2. I thank you Lord for your mercy.
3. Confess your sins before the Lord and repent of them.
4. I pray that you forgive me all my sins of mismanaging the resources you have entrusted in my care.

5. Thou spirit of Mormon fighting over the resources of God in the area of my finances, be destroyed in the name of Jesus.

6. Rivers of gold from the throne of grace flow into my life in the name of Jesus.

7. My father, satisfy me with your riches of gold in the name of Jesus.

8. Virtuous money-generating ideas, come into my mind in the name of Jesus.

9. Wealth-generating ideas, come into my mind in the name of Jesus.

10. Mechanical problems wired against my finances, perish in the name of Jesus.

11. Every spirit plundering my divine ideas, be consumed by the fire of God in the name of Jesus.

12. Every power or spirit, setting confusion into my mind, is cast out and consumed by the fire of God in the name of Jesus.

13. Every power or spirit causing drought in the midst of my plenty, your time is up, power of God,

14. My life you have no other option than to move forward, therefore by the power in the name of Jesus and resurrection, I move forward for good in the name of Jesus.

15. Every rag, dirty clothes, clothes of disgust covering my glory, the Lord destroys you by His consuming fire, and I am set free in the name of Jesus.

16. Every power that is letting me waste our labor, perish by fire in the name of Jesus.

17. I will not work for another person to eat in the name of Jesus.

18. Every desert season in my life is over, I enter into the season of fruitfulness in the name of Jesus.

19. Every one of my blessings stolen from me by demonic reptiles, be restored in the name of Jesus.

20.   The spirit of slow progress in my life, perish in the name of Jesus.

21. I receive the overtakers' anointing in the name of Jesus.

22.O Lord, take me out of the desert land to a place of prosperity in the name of Jesus.

23.Joy is my portion this year in the name of Jesus.

24.Profitability is my portion in the name of Jesus.

25.I come against every abortion of dreams and finance in the name of Jesus.

26.   My heavens, open up for the showers of blessings in the name of Jesus

27. My heavens, let it rain upon my destiny in the name of Jesus.

28.Every iron cloud, metallic ceiling holding me down, limiting how high to how I can go, break by fire in the name of Jesus.

29.Every power preventing me from having sufficient monetary resources (the spirit of living from paycheck to paycheck), the fire of God destroys you in the name of Jesus.

30. Funds from heaven flow into my hands and bank account in the name of Jesus.

31. I receive the anointing to run businesses successfully in the name of Jesus.

32. Every demonic tower of deception in my foundation, that has vowed to keep me in a dungeon of financial distress, collapse and perish in Jesus Name.

33. The power that profits from business, from divine ideas, come upon my destinies in Jesus Name

34. Powers to profit from divine ideas locate my destiny in Jesus Name.

35. Lord, disgrace the chief principality warring against my finances in Jesus Name.

36. Thou destiny thief, take your hands off God's property entrusted in my care, in Jesus Name.

37. Destiny thieves, over my finances and properties, perish in the name of Jesus.

38. Every demonic power, beckoning my spirit for slavery and poverty, perish in Jesus Name.

39. All of my foreign benefits, be restored to me in Jesus Name.

40. Holy Spirit, overshadow my finances in Jesus Name.

41. Thou spirit of confusion that turns people from greatness to nothingness, my life is not your candidate.

42. Lord, I receive the spirit of accuracy and focus from above in Jesus Name.

43. I will not die with wonders and glory in the name of Jesus.

44. Every of my divinely inspired ideas, already in the grave, be resurrected by the fire of God in Jesus Name

45. My father, revive every divinely inspired idea that has been dead in my life, in the name of Jesus.

46. O heavens unleash the angels of radical blessings upon my life.

47. (Call upon the name of Jesus seven times and pray..) - By the power that

established the sun and moon, that they never conflict against each other, my glory begins to shine in the name of Jesus.

48. Every ancient closet housing my milk and honey, give it up and return back to me Jesus Name.

49. Every shackle making it difficult to move forward financially, be broken in the name of Jesus.

50. Powers tying the rope of backwardness against my moving forward, Lord, arise in your anger and waste them in the name of Jesus.

51. All forms of aggressive poverty biting or gripping my breakthrough, Lord utterly disgrace them publicly and destroy them in the name of Jesus.

52. Every wandering spirit plaquing my destiny, your time is up perish by fire in the name of Jesus.

53. Every zigzag progress, one leg forward, 10 steps backward plaquing my destiny, be destroyed by fire in the name of Jesus.

54. Kingly anointing in my life begins to manifest in the name of Jesus.

55. Every gathering of demonic elders that has dug a secret hole against my destiny, hiding my resources and virtues in that hole, the thunder of God, shatter the demonic elders and their holes and retrieve my stolen virtues unto me in the name of Jesus.

56. Every power auctioning off your glory, the Lord disgraces that power.

57. My belongings that are being auctioned, I put an end to that auction and recover you in the name of Jesus.

58. Let my life be the benchmark of excellence in the name of Jesus.

59. Every power of empty promises plaquing my destiny, perish in the name of Jesus.

60. Every power of slippery breakthroughs, lose your hold over my destiny in the name of Jesus.

61. Power of desolation working in my life, perish in the name of Jesus.

62.   Every web of setbacks against my life and destiny, perish in the name of Jesus.

63.   Every mara water in the journey of my destiny shall be destroyed in the name of Jesus.

64. My life, move forward for good in Jesus Name.

65. My father, set me apart, make me the preferred choice in Jesus Name.

66.   My father in business, make my product the preferred product in the name of Jesus.

67. My father, when positive life changing decisions need to be made, make the preferred choice in the name of Jesus

68.   My spirit man awakes from slumber in the name of Jesus

69.   On the day of my appointment with destiny, I will not be asleep in Jesus Name.

70. I am set up on high above every contender in the name of Jesus

71. I am set up on high above every competitor in the name of Jesus

72. Divine resources, flow into my stewardship in Jesus Name.

73. Let my life be the recipient of your promotion this week in Jesus Name.

74. My father set me on high in the name of Jesus.

75. Destiny thief over our freedom, perish in the name of Jesus.

76. I will not lose the sweetness in my life in the name of Jesus.

77. Cycle of stagnancy in my career is ended by the Right Hand of the Lord, in the name of Jesus

78. Opposition to the move of God in my finances is consumed by the fire of the Lord in the name of Jesus.

79. My father, the one who molded me and knows me, pour your sweetness upon my life in Jesus Name.

80. Spirits of insights and foresight come upon me in the name of Jesus.

81. The covenant of poverty has ended in the name of Jesus.

82. Thou spirit of Hiel, attempting to rebuild all the strongholds of financial failure in my life, you are rendered impotent and cursed forever in Jesus Name

83. Afflictions shall rise no more because I seal my prayers with the blood of Jesus and the fire of the Holy Spirit.

84. Glory and honor be to you Lord Jesus for answered prayers.

JOURNAL

9

DELIVERANCE OF THE BRAIN & MIND

"Guard your heart above all else, for it determines the course of your life"
Proverbs 4:23

The mind and brain are used interchangeably in this book. Your mind is the laboratory, where all that you would do and become is born. If you are able to win the battle of your mind, you have gained an advantage in life. The reason is that every single activity from the day you were born, to the day you'll leave this world, is planted and nurtured from the right mind.

If the battle in your mind is not lost, the battle in your life is not over. Whatever you do, be sure to guard your heart.

HOW MIND ATTACK WORKS

The devil understands the power of the mind and has extensively used it against many. Some of the devil's tools of mind manipulation include doubts, fear, ignorance, sadness and negative.

Doubt, Fear, Discouragement

You are suddenly inspired and have a brilliant idea. You think about it and it is mindblowing. Suddenly, a thought creeps in and whispers, "what makes you think you can accomplish that", "who has ever reached this height in your family". You confide in your friends and one of them say, "how could that be possible", you begin to nurture doubts and fear, and guess what, you let it go. Those are examples of how people have lost the battles of their minds.

Distraction Through Social Media

While you can benefit from using social media technologies, be very careful what you feed your mind from there as well. Apart from wasting your time, be alert spiritually, and stay away from contents that corrupt the spirit and could potentially create a baggage of filth in your mind.

Negativity

If you master how to avoid negativity, you have mastered how to nurture the goldmine in your mind. Negativity is one tool that has been used to attack the mind. It is subtle and looks harmless. It is the killer of joy and stealer of goodness. It multiplies sorrow and affliction. Negative words are evil prophecies and should be avoided. You should not allow negative people, worry, anxiety, or fear to control your mind or speak into your world. These are internal agents of the devil that are activated in people to make them self-destruct.

Other mind killers

Whatever you do, watch after your brain. There are so many exercises people do that kill their brains daily. People are often taught how to speak eloquently, and how to communicate, but not taught how to listen. Engaging in activities that help the brain such as reading is a must-do for people who want to live above average. As believers, you are called to be the salt of the world, to shine forth, so that the glory of God is reflected upon your life. In order to do this, you must master how to use the brain that the Lord has given you at an optimal level.

Whatever you feed your brain. If you feed your brain fear, it'll multiply anxiety, and chaos will be the order of the day. These are subtle tactics used by the enemy. Never let the enemy prophesy into your mind through discouragement, fear, doubt or sadness. Do not foster the suggestions of the enemy. With joy you will conquer many spiritual battles. Remember, unpleasant atmospheres are rarely blessed.

When the enemy floods your mind with negativity, connect with the spirit of God and let Him raise standards. Your responses to situations are a reflection of the state of the mind. Watch out that this is not your portion, that you do not partake in all these things.

Transforming your mind

Look for ways to feed your brain godly information so that it multiplies wisdom unto you, and you can impact your community. The Lord has called you to be a chosen generation, not a complacent or mediocre one. Now is the time and opportunity for you to enter into the new realm of possibilities and power that the Lord has released unto your brain. If you will take a moment to ask, the

Lord will give unto you, but you also have roles to play:

1. Stay steady and positive. Never allow the devil to push your mind into seasons of joy and sadness, encouragement and discouragement, let your mind be at a constant season of joy.

2. Respond to every situation with joy and gladness.

3. Let your joy know no bound.

4. Never echo the voice of darkness, even when things are not going great.

5. Take charge of the atmosphere with the higher authority in you.

PRAYERS FOR DELIVERANCE OF THE MIND & BRAIN

- Confess and repent from all your sins.
- Build a life and relationship with the Lord.

Worship
- Build a worship altar to the Lord

Spend 12 minutes in worship before you say the prayers.

Personalize and meditate on the following scriptures:

"Do not conform to the pattern of this world, but be transformed by the renewing of your mind. Then you will be able to test and approve what God's will is—his good, pleasing and perfect will" Romans 12:2

"Finally, brothers and sisters, whatever is true, whatever is noble, whatever is right, whatever is pure, whatever is lovely, whatever is admirable—if anything is excellent or

praiseworthy—think about such things". Philippians 4:8

"We demolish arguments and every pretension that sets itself up against the knowledge of God, and we take captive every thought to make it obedient to Christ" 2 Corinthians 10:5

"Above all else, guard your heart, for everything you do flows from it" Proverbs 4:23

Lay your hands upon your head and decree:

1. My brain receives deliverance from death.
2. For I have the mind of Christ, every connection in my brain that has not been used and is dying, be revived by the resurrection power of the Lord.
3. My brain, receive deliverance from death in Jesus Name.
4. I receive the power of heavenly imagination in Jesus Name.
5. My brain, receive the awakening of God in Jesus Name.
6. My brain, arise and wake up in Jesus Name.

7. My brain, receive the ability to function at your maximum level in Jesus Name.

8. My brain, receive the gift of foresight and insight in Jesus Name.

9. Every dead cell, every information bearing cell that is dead in my brain, come back to life in the name of Jesus.

10. For every dead cell, Lord create more in the name of Jesus.

11. Heavenly empowerment, be released upon my brain in Jesus name.

12. Every power that besieged my brain, that has blocked good things from coming in and going out, perish in Jesus Name.

13. Demonic arrows into my brain, get out and go back with fire to your senders in the name of Jesus.

14. My father, every power that is frying my brain, on a demonic frying pan, with demonic fire, thunder of God, strike them and set my brain free in Jesus' name.

15. Lord, reinvent my brain in Jesus name.

16. Every demonic transplant of my brain,

being used in demonic computing factory, fire of the Holy Ghost, set my brain free and set the demonic factory on ablaze in Jesus Name.

17. Every power firing evil arrows of failure into my brain, perish in your own wickedness in the name of Jesus.

18. O Lord, let your fresh breath blow right now over my brain in Jesus Name.

19. Demonic brain rental program - my brain is not your candidate, my brain is not susceptible to your rental program, perish in the name of Jesus.

20. Every demonic sequencing transmitting death, my brain is not your victim, my brain is fortified by the power in the name of Jesus.

21. My mind, be delivered from the rottenness of perdition in the name of Jesus.

22. Every information mismatch arrow fired into my brain, locate your senders and destroy them in the name of Jesus.

23. Thou demonic power and curse that

seizes glory, preventing me from enjoying my glory, I reject you, perish by fire in the name of Jesus.

24. Every power of destructive imagination against my mind is consumed by the fire of the Holy Spirit, in the name of Jesus.

25. Every power of destructive imagination that has taken hold of my mind, perishes in the name of Jesus.

26. Every arrow of confusion and insanity fired into my brain, I pull you out and gather you with the finger of God, I send you right back to your senders in the name of Jesus.

27. Every demonic power that is siphoning my brain, to prevent the power and knowledge of God from flowing into my mind, be destroyed in the name of Jesus.

28. Every power that wants to turn my brain into the sole of my feet, like an object of ridicule, my life is not your candidate, perish in the name of Jesus.

29. Every power of mind blankness against my mind, perishes in the name of Jesus.

30. My mind, you are powerful, you are strong, you are not a loser in the name of Jesus.

31. My mind, you are the mind of Christ, wake up in the name of Jesus.

32. Every mind-choking thorn, at work in my mind, at work in my life, be consumed by fire in the name of Jesus

33. Every destructive suggestion from the pit of hell, displacing God's creative process in my mind, be destroyed in the name of Jesus.

34. Every demonic nail, nailed into my ear, into my mind to prevent me from hearing the voice of God, to not receive heavenly transmission, be uprooted by fire, in the name of Jesus.

35. Thou organ between my ears (my brain), I rededicate you to the Lord Jesus.

36. Every demonic role reversal against my mind to function hazardly, be nullified and destroyed by the power in the name of Jesus.

37. Every wasting tactic of the enemy against my mind, to disgrace my destiny, be exposed, be disgraced and be destroyed in Jesus Name.

38. Thou scheme of Babylon against my destiny, be wasted by the consuming fire in the name of Jesus.

39. Thou babylonic scheme against my mind, be wasted by the fire of the Holy Ghost in Jesus Name..

40. Every demonic helmet, designed to hinder my mind from hearing from the Lord Jesus, to keep me away from hearing from heaven, be melted by fire in the name of Jesus.

41. Every demonic roll call of borrowed minds, working in demonic camps, my mind does not belong to your register, perish in the name of Jesus.

42. Every demonic infinite loop of death, my brain is not your victim, perish in the name of Jesus.

43. Every arrow of infirmity fired into my brain, get out now and locate your sender in the name of Jesus.

44. Thou demonic remote control that wants to control my mind, you have no hold over my mind in the name of Jesus.

45. Every power pouring the demonic oil of backwardness upon my brain, to alter my consciousness, to make my brain sleep where and when it's supposed to be active, power and thunder of God destroys you in the name of Jesus.

46. Every demonic arrow fired into my life and destiny, by proximity, locate your sender for destruction.

47. Thou spirit of regression, be cast out of my mind in the name of Jesus.

48. My mind will not fall out of place in the name of Jesus.

49. All assault of darkness against my mind is canceled by the blood of Jesus, in the name of Jesus.

50. My mind shall not be a casualty of war, in the name of Jesus.

51. Satanic covenant of paralysis upon my mind is canceled by the blood of Jesus, be broken by the blood of Jesus

52. Satanic covenant of blankness upon my mind is canceled by the blood of Jesus, be broken by the blood of Jesus

53. Satanic covenant of degradation upon my mind is canceled by the blood of Jesus, be broken by the blood of Jesus

54. Powers of mind controllers over my mind are null and void in the name of Jesus.

55. covenant of degradation upon my mind is canceled by the blood of Jesus, be broken by the blood of Jesus

56. Fire of God, scatter the devices of the crafty over my mind, in the name of Jesus.

57. Scatter the devices of the crafty over my marriage

58. My mind shall not be scattered in the name of Jesus.

59. Demonic domination over my mind is uprooted and burned to ashes by the

consuming fire of God in the name of Jesus.

60. My mind is not the habitation of darkness in the name of Jesus

61. Demons in my mind, get out in the name of Jesus.

62. Demons of filthiness in my mind, get out in the name of Jesus

63. Demons of forgetfulness in my mind, get out in the name of Jesus.

64. Demons arresting my mind for witchcraft control, get out by the fire of the Holy Spirit in the name of Jesus.

65. All the implantation of anger in my mind is uprooted in the name of Jesus.

66. Hands of darkness, wiping out memory from my mind, the consuming fire of God burns you in the name of Jesus.

67. I expel the activities of demons and darkness in my mind in the name of Jesus of that demon in the environment.

68. Let the east wind of God blow away the evil participants in my marriage in the name of Jesus

69. The power of the strange entity sitting upon my in the name of Jesus

70. The arguments and strong points of darkness over my mind have no hold any longer, therefore, all demonic powers, lose your hold over my mind in the name of Jesus.

71. Affliction has no place in my mind in the name of Jesus.

72. My mind shall not be bewitched in the name of Jesus

73. Control of darkness has no hold over my mind in the name of Jesus.

74. Powers sent to dry up my mind is swallowed by the earth in the name of Jesus.

75. Let the spirit of fear holding my mind down be conquered in the name of Jesus

76. The ship of my life shall not be sunken in the name of Jesus

77. The yoke of addiction over my mind is broken in the name of Jesus

78. Powers speaking death and damnation over my mind, receive instant condemnation in the name of Jesus.

79. Confusion shall not locate my mind in the name of Jesus.

80. No longer shall my mind be susceptible to the manipulation of darkness in the name of Jesus.

81. My mind is delivered from the spirit of error, in the name of Jesus.

82. Powers placing unending yokes and unreasonable demands over my life are destroyed in the name of Jesus.

83. Snares of darkness set for my mind shall fail in the name of Jesus.

84. I receive freshness and the renewal of mind in the name of Jesus.

85. Lord Jesus, cleanse my mind with the purest oil from your presence in the name of Jesus.

86. Lord, anoint my mind for the journey ahead, in the name of Jesus.

87. Lord, let the power of God that cannot be ridiculed overshadow my mind in the name of Jesus.

88. My mind, receive the breath of God's life in the name of Jesus

89. My mind receives the resurrection power of God, in the name of Jesus.

90. Blessed is my mind, as God is in my thoughts in the name of Jesus.

91. I retain the knowledge of the Lord in my mind in the name of Jesus.

92. I receive healing in the mind in the name of Jesus.

93. I cover my mind with the blood of Jesus.

94. Afflictions shall rise no more because I seal my prayers with the blood of Jesus and the fire of the Holy Spirit.

95. My mind receives the light of God, in the name of Jesus.

96. Glory and honor be to you Lord Jesus for answered prayers.

JOURNAL

10

DELIVERANCE OF DESTINY

"For I know the plans that I have for you,' declares the LORD, '
plans for welfare and not for calamity to give you a future and
a hope"
Jeremiah 29:11

Your destiny is the reason you are here, to fulfill God's assignment for your life. If you are a Jonah, I'll say unto you, get out of the boat and head to your place of assignment. Enough of traveling the roads that do not lead to your destination.

You can tell a destiny is malformed or corrupted if you see the following symptoms in the life of an individual. Those who are supposed to be leaders remain in servitude, students who are always learning and never understanding, workers who are always working hard and never yielding good fruits, people having no concrete relationship with the Lord, ministers of the gospel relying on stale revelations given to others, having no direct revelations of their own, studying the scripture never knowing or living the way of the Lord.

THE MYSTERY OF DESTINY

What is the use of a tasteless salt, what is the use of a lamp without a light? What is the use of the sun without shine? This is the illustration of a christian life that is not going according to God's plan. Until believers rise up to fulfill that scripture "become the salt of the earth", will there be taste in their lives? What benefit is a salt that has lost its flavor? Believers today are being trampled under foot because their lives have lost its flavor. If you are not fulfilling God's plan for your life to its maximum, your destiny is delivering short of God's glory.

A destiny under bondage can be likened to a malformed vessel. Some vessels have knowingly or unknowingly walked away from their original purpose. These vessels have fled or been displaced from their place of assignment. When there is a deviation from your divine assignment, it opens you up to attacks. If you are a present day Jonah who has wandered away or neglected your divine assignment, the boat is about to capsize, get off the boat. You need to head back to your original assignment in order not to destroy innocent lives attached to your destiny.

THE OUTCOME OF YOUR DESTINY

Two major factors that determine the outcome of your destiny are discussed here. They will either alter your destiny positively or negatively are your background and your sphere of influence.

Your Background

Your family of origin, your lineage, where you come from may be a blessing or a curse to your destiny. Here's a revelation I received from the Lord.

On the day a child is born, they receive a bag from their family. Some families give their newborn a full bag, while others pass on an empty bag. Inside the full bags are heavy yokes of generational issues that have gone unresolved. The concept of the full bag plays differently in every family. Some families pass on debts to their children, some pass on evil family patterns, or unresolved spiritual issues..

In families who know the ways of the Lord, they pass on empty bags to their newborns. As those children grow, the word of God is being deposited in the empty bags and the children learn the ways of the Lord. That's why children from homes built on the true

Word of God are able to run faster in life to fulfill their destinies.

Your Sphere of Influence are the people you meet and connect with in the journey of your life. They can be grouped into destiny killers and destiny helpers.

DESTINY KILLERS

As the name implies, they cause death to destinies. Destiny killers ruin God's purposes in the lives of their victims. They distract and derail from the divine path leading to a divine destination. They show up in everyday lives.

Wrong Alliances

An ally is a wrong one if they move against God's will in your life. The wrong alliances are people with opposing visions as you and they could mar the purpose of God for your life.. They come as time wasters, friends with benefits, unmarried sexual partners, gossip buddies, persons inspired by adulterous spirits whose goal is to lure you from the ways of the Lord.

"Later, Jehoshaphat king of Judah made an alliance with Ahaziah king of Israel, whose ways were wicked".
2 Chronicles 20:35

False prophets

There was the case of a woman who shared with us that a prophet told her to marry an unbeliever. She went ahead to marry the unbeliever, and 36 years later she is still living in bondage in her marriage. After prayers and ministry to her, she dreamed that the Lord delivered her from a goat. She continues to pray for her husband to be saved. She began to have revelations that she had married the wrong person, but it was too late. The person who prophesied to her lured her away from God's plan for her life was her destiny killer.

"For false messiahs and false prophets will appear and perform great signs and wonders to deceive, if possible, even the elect"
Matthew 24:24

A lot of people have been bound under these yokes of false prophets. Their victims have fallen into marital disasters, financial prisons, and all sorts of bondages because they fell into their traps of destiny destruction. Some are bible teachers who tweak the word of God, and tell you to disobey the word of God without using the word "disobedience".

DESTINY HELPERS

Mentors

The divine mentor who walks your journey with you, shares their useful experiences with you, so that you don't have to learn through your own experiences. They save you time and can help you expedite the fulfillment of your destiny.

Divine Connectors

They hold the keys to the secrets of your liberation. The Lord has given them the links to your breakthrough. They have the keys to vital information that you need to advance in life. God uses to connect potential spouses, businesses contracts, and

How the Enemy Attacks Divine helpers

The enemy uses critical strategies to destroy people's relationships with their destiny helpers. The enemy's goal is to send the wrong message to their destiny helpers and prevent a divine assignment from being carried out .

Some attacks are launched such that people never meet their destiny helpers. A simple tactic the enemy sends spirits like anger to dwell in the lives of their people. The enemy remotely activates the anger system to be in full effect at appointed times when the host is about to come in contact with their destiny helpers. For some, it could be the spirit of distraction, impatience, restlessness, ineffective communication. For some, the spirit of confusion is set in motion, causing divine helpers to be perceived as enemies and destiny killers as friends.

FULFILLING YOUR DESTINY

If your destiny has been compromised, the solution is to submit yourself to be under the mighty hands of the Lord. Only the Lord can remold you, no matter how bad you think it is. When you go back to the Lord in repentance, He takes you through a process of pruning which can be painful to your flesh. This process is indeed painful but worth enduring. He inserts you into fire, melts you down and peels off impurities. All the parasites attached to your destiny will be taken out and you will be reshaped for noble use. Part of this process is that the Lord may ask you to cut off certain relationships that have caused obstruction to your destiny. Do not be sentimental about it so you don't put your destiny at stake. This means you will submit to the Lord to write the upcoming chapters of your life, while you read the script in obedience.

"Therefore, I urge you, brothers and sisters, in view of God's mercy, to offer your bodies as a living sacrifice, holy and pleasing to God—this is your true and proper

worship. Do not conform to the pattern of this world, but be transformed by the renewing of your mind. Then you will be able to test and approve what God's will is—his good, pleasing and perfect will"

Romans 12:1-2

PRAYERS FOR THE DELIVERANCE OF DESTINY

- Confess and repent from all your sins.
- Build a life and relationship with the Lord.

Worship

- Build a worship altar to the Lord

Spend 12 minutes in worship before you say the prayers.

Personalize and meditate on the following Scriptures:

"You are the salt of the earth; but if the salt loses its flavor, how shall it be seasoned? It is then good for nothing but to be thrown out and trampled underfoot by men. "You are the light of the world. A city that is set on a hill cannot be hidden.Nor do they light a lamp and put it under a basket, but on a lampstand, and it gives light to all who are in the house. Let your light so shine before men, that they may see your good works and glorify your Father in heaven."

Matthew 5:13-16

1. My father, Let the salt that you have made me, never lose its flavor in the name of Jesus.

2. Any demonic annexation of any portion of my destiny, lose your hold in the name of Jesus.

3. Every garment of sorrow put upon my destiny or inherited be burned to death in Jesus Name.

4. Profitless hard labor, my life is not your candidate, perish in the name of Jesus.

5. Stolen ladder of my ascension to prosperity, to breakthrough, where art thou, be restored unto me by fire in the name of Jesus.

6. Thou popcorn miracle, my life is not your victim, lasting miracle my life is ready, make my life your habitation in the name of Jesus.

7. Every power using applause and false humility to ruin my destiny, let the

thunder of God destroy them in the name of Jesus.

8. Every demonic official trap/proposal/argument against your destiny, it is nullified by the blood of Jesus.

9. Every arrow of shame and disgrace fired into my destiny and family, backfire in the name of Jesus.

10. Every of my destiny that has been stuck in the well of life is released to me in the name of Jesus.

11. My destiny, my blessing and resources buried deep in the belly of the earth, by the power of the most High come up to me, in Jesus Name.

12. By the power that established the sun, the moon and star, every of my benefits and resources that have been attacked by the power of the sun, moon and star, be released in Jesus Name.

13. My Father, elevate my life like that of a unicorn, in the name of Jesus.

14. My life get out of deficit, my life get out of rot, abundance is your portion in the name of Jesus.

15. Every curse of thou shall not prosper, every curse of thou shall not prosper, working against my destiny, be broken by the blood of Jesus.

16. Every curse from glory to doom, curse from glory to failure that has plagued my ancestors, that has plagued my family line, that wants to make my life its next candidate, my life is not your candidate, be broken by the blood of Jesus.

17. Thou demonic power and curse that seizes glory and borrows glory such that the owner of the glory never enjoys benefits from their glory, my life rejects you, perish by fire in the name of Jesus.

18. Every power pouring the demonic oil of backwardness upon my destiny, thunder of God, strike them dead in the name of Jesus.

19. Every power that has defecated upon my destiny, the Lord disgraces and destroys your power in the name of Jesus.

20. Every time that I have done things that have translated into defecting upon my own destiny, O Lord have mercy in the name of Jesus.

21. Every time that I have exposed my destiny to the hands of the enemy, O Lord deliver me and my destiny in the name of Jesus.

22. My portion is removed from every evil box in the name of Jesus

23. Lord, expose and destroy the enemy's ambush against my destiny, in Jesus Name.

24. All my foreign benefits, it is time for your manifestation, locate me without delay, in the name of Jesus.

25. My blessings from the north, east, west, locate me without delay in the name of Jesus.

26. Manifestation of witchcraft hand,

against my destiny on earth, consume them in the name of Jesus.

27. Every demonic hand, every witchcraft hand, against my life, manipulating my destiny, wither away in the name of Jesus.

28. Every strange woman or woman, any owner of strange hand upon my destiny, be destroyed by the fire of God in the name of Jesus.

29. Every demonic gathering of the enemy against my life, against my destiny, perish in the name of Jesus.

30. Every cricket army against my destiny, fire of the Holy Ghost consume them in the name of Jesus.

31. Every rubbish anointing contending against my destiny, contending against the power of God against my life, be exposed be disgraced in the name Jesus.

32. Every spirit of emptiness that has attached itself to me, to siphon all of my virtues into an empty vessel/container,

be exposed, be disgraced and destroyed by the fire of God in the name of Jesus.

33.Every power of empty promises plaquing my destiny, your time is up, perish in the name of Jesus.

34.Every power of slippery breakthroughs, lose your hold over my destiny in the name of jesus.

35.Thou perfect storm and disaster, set to bring my destiny to rubles, you have failed, perish in the name of Jesus.

36.   My father, Let the salt that you have made me, never lose its flavor in Jesus Name

37. Salt of my destiny, flavor up in Jesus Name.

38.The flavor of God that makes the gentiles open their mouth in utter amazement, in shocking surprise for good, at what God is doing in my life, descend upon my life, in the name of Jesus

39.Heaven, open up and favor me.

40.   Every demonic baggage placed upon my destiny from my family of origin,

my life is no longer your candidate, be destroyed, by fire of the Holy Ghost.

41. My Father, give me an understanding of the times I live in.

42. My Father, give me a spiritual understanding of the times I live in.

43. My Father, give me a physical understanding of the times I live in.

44. My Father, give me a mental understanding of the time I live in.

45. My Father, give me an emotional understanding of the times that I live in

46. Power that makes people become last, the power of the least over my destiny, perish in the name of Jesus.

47. Power of the Most High God, deliver me from every chain holding me back from reaching your goal for my life.

48. I will move forward in this year, in the name of Jesus

49. Every truncated wealth in the past year, in this year, you shall no longer be truncated, let there be a year of explosive growth over my life in Jesus Name.

50. Mysteries of my kingly inheritance shall be manifest to me in the name of Jesus Name.

51. Inheritance thieves, my life is not your victim, perish in the name of Jesus.

52. Every thieves of my inheritance in Christ, perish in the name of Jesus

53. Thou giant plunderers, you can not plunder my life, plunder yourself and perish in the name of Jesus.

54. Thou weeping deceiver over my destiny, perish in the name of Jesus

55. Thou disguising plunderer, over my destiny, you can no longer plunder me, because I belong to the Lord Jesus, perish in the name of Jesus.

56. Thou deceiver plunderer over our inheritance, you cannot plunder me, perish in the name of Jesus.

57. Thou deceiver plunderer over my children, you cannot plunder my children, perish in the name of Jesus.

58. Thou deceiver plunderer over our finances, you cannot plunder me, perish in the name of Jesus.

59. Thou deceiver plunderer over my future , you cannot plunder me, perish in the name of Jesus

60. Mechanical problems, wired against my destiny, my life is not your victim, perish in Jesus Name.

61. Thou isguising plunderer against destiny, by the power in the name of Jesus, you are cursed with a curse, in the name of Jesus - Joshua 9:23

62. Powers using fear to displace me from my place of promotion and breakthroughs are destroyed in the name of Jesus.

63. Every good thing that is dead in my life, by the resurrection power of the Lord, come back to life in the name of Jesus

64. Every demonic gathering of demonic elders, beating demonic drums, against

my destiny, life, by the Lord's thunder, perish in the name of Jesus.

65. Every power that wants to make me weep and live in regrets in my old age, the Lord nullifies you in the name of Jesus.

66. Let the purity of God sanctify the Holy Ground of my destiny in the name of Jesus.

67. Every battle that wants to pair me with destiny destroyers, perish by fire in the name of Jesus

68. Every enchantment made against my name and destiny, be nullified by the blood of Jesus.

69. Every power sitting on my destiny, sending curses upon my destiny, thunder of God, unseat them and destroy them in the name of Jesus.

70. Every curse of revenge, crying day and night before the Lord, against my life and destiny, blood of Jesus, mercy of God, speak for me in the name of Jesus.

71. Every demonic attack against my star, be quenched by the fire of God in the name of Jesus.

72. Every power of the enemy to disgrace our destiny, perish by fire in the name of Jesus

73. I come against every accidental gun fire in the name of Jesus

74. Our destinies will not be wasted in the name of Jesus.

75. Our destiny will not be cut short in the name of Jesus.

76. Every power of excess baggage against my destiny, the Lord disgraces them and cuts ties from me in Jesus Name.

77. Every dirt, trouble that has been tied into my destiny, I sever ties with them with the blazing sword of the Lord in the name of Jesus.

78. My destiny will not be locked up in demonic prison in the name of Jesus.

79. Every demonic elephant assigned to me, that makes the most simple task difficult,

fire of God, consume such elephant and I am set free in the name of Jesus.

80. I will not live my life in shame, in the name of Jesus.

81. I will not live my life in loneliness in the name of Jesus.

82. I will not live my life in dejection in the name of Jesus.

83. I will not live my life in rejection in the name of Jesus.

84. The lamp of my destiny will not be snuffed out, in the name of Jesus.

85. The star of my destiny, shine in the name of Jesus.

86. Every glory stealer, my glory is not your victim, perish in the name of Jesus.

87. Jesus, Alpha and Omega, locate me, set me free in the name of Jesus.

88. Every demonic arrow, fired against the voice of my destiny, backfire in the name of Jesus.

89. Every xray of darkness against my destiny, against my health, be destroyed in the name of Jesus.

90. Every battle of mistaken identity that has been fighting my destiny, be nullified by the blood of Jesus, in the name of Jesus.

91. Every manifestation of the orphan spirit in my destiny, lose your hold over my destiny in Jesus Name.

92. Every power that has added my name to the wrong family tree, to the demonic family tree, Lord fight for me, and cut my name free.

93. Every hexagonal battle, confronting my destiny, perish in the name of Jesus.

94. Every time-sensitive missile, that has been tied to my destiny, be dismantled by the fire of the God of Elijah.

95. The portion of my virtues stolen from me , be restored by the power in the blood of Jesus.

96. Every demonic gathering of demonic elders, fanning the flame of trouble, evil over my life, what are you waiting for, perish by fire in the name of Jesus.

97. Every power of evil tongue, set to crush my destiny, let the voice of the Most High silence them forever in the name of Jesus.

98. Every arrow of shame and disgrace fired into my life, get out of my life and go back to your sender in the name of Jesus.

99. Every crooked foundation, every faulty foundation, Holy spirit repairs them.

100. My voice, captured in a demonic coven, be set free in the name of Jesus.

101. Every demonic masked man, tormenting my destiny, to keep me in slavery, perish in the name of Jesus.

102. Every ancient secret holding the keys to my deliverance, be revealed to me in the name of jesus.

103. Thou demonic friendly jailor that has been in charge of my imprisonment, be exposed and destroyed in the name of Jesus.

104. Let the voice of my destiny, roar back to life in the name of Jesus.

105. Put your seal of protection upon my destiny, mark my life with your seal in the name of Jesus

106. Every of my foreign benefits, locate me speedily in the name of Jesus

107. Lord, energize my inner man to be always ready for battle in the name of Jesus.

108. Each of my glories, buried in mud, come out and be refined by the fire of the Lord.

109. Every deception in my circle, be exposed and disgraced in the name of Jesus.

110. Yahweh, thou defender of the defenseless, defend my existence in the name of Jesus.

111. Voice of my destiny, roar back to life in the name of Jesus.

112. Powers manipulating and truncating my destiny, using the seed of my infancy to afflict me, let the fire of the God of

Elijah consume them in the name of Jesus.

113. The yoke of unprofitable certificates over your certificates and skills is broken in the name of Jesus.

114. Every demonic belt of hardship, tied to my waist to manipulate my destiny, shatter by fire in the name of Jesus

115. My life get out of deficit, abundance is your portion.

116. Every of my destiny kept and hidden in the grave, be released unto my in the name of Jesus.

117. My royal garment that has been soiled, my royal garment that has been buried in shame and disgrace, blood of Jesus, wash it clean in the name of Jesus. Come back to life by the blood of Jesus.

118. On the day of my joy and glory, I will not be found wanting.

119. The broken key of my destiny, O Lord, restore with your right hand in the name of Jesus.

120. Thou destiny helper that has forgotten me, let the hands of the Lord connect us and quicken your spirit to remember me for good in the name of Jesus.

121. Every power that is coveting my destiny, Lord disgrace and nullify their power in the name of Jesus.

122. Lord Jesus, elevate the status of my destiny in the name of Jesus.

123. Lord Jesus, elevate my glory in the name of Jesus

124. Thou Helper of my destiny, let scales be removed from my face that I may wake up to begin your assignment in my life in the name of Jesus.

125. Every aggressive afflictor of my destiny, by the power of God, I drag you to the court of the Lord, receive judgment in the name of Jesus.

126. Demonic mask covering my destiny, be removed by the resurrection power of Jesus.

127. I will not pack my enemy along with me into my promised land in the name of Jesus

128. Afflictions shall rise no more because I seal my prayers with the blood of Jesus and the fire of the Holy Spirit.

129. Glory and honor be to you Lord Jesus for answered prayers.

JOURNAL

11

FOUNDATIONAL

DELIVERANCE

When the foundations are being destroyed, what can
the righteous do?"
Psalms 11:3

Your foundation will make or mar you.
Unresolved issues flow through generations.
The revelation of certain secrets holds the key

to your deliverance. You need to conduct a spiritual research on your foundation. It is called Spiritual mapping. Spiritual mapping is gathering spiritual intelligence about your foundation.

Personal Deliverance Story

In the place of prayers, the Lord had told us to pray strange prayers like *"Every power that has planted my name to the wrong family tree, let my name be uprooted"*. It looked weird, but from what I have learned, I have learned just to obey the Lord. After praying, I heard the Lord say to me, "who is your father"?. It was not the first time the Holy Spirit had asked me similar questions, but I had ignored it for long. This time, I listened and wanted to know more.

I began to ask questions and found that the person whom I grew up to know as my father, is not my father. It was a case of an abortion that was thought to be successful. This revelation was the answer to the prayer given in the place of prayers: *"Every power that has planted my name to the wrong family tree, let my name be uprooted.* Prior to this revelation, I did not realize my life and family had been built under the wrong family tree.

Until you understand your foundation, would you be able to deploy customized prayers towards your specific situation. The lack of understanding of foundation is the reason why people pray amiss. A symptom may appear and the symptom is being treated with prayers without addressing the major disease.

HOW TO GATHER SPIRITUAL INTELLIGENCE

We are in the times where the Holy Spirit is fully functional and will abide with anyone who does the will of the Father. You will be surprised when you begin to ask these questions and the kind of answers you will receive. You need to begin to ask the Holy Spirit questions like:

- Who sinned, is it I or my parents?
- What is the secret to the foundation of

my life?

- What is the spiritual atmosphere in my foundation?

- What is my inheritance from my earthly parents?

- What are the major trends in my father's house?

- What are the major trends in my mother's house ?

EXAMPLES OF FOUNDATIONAL BONDAGES

Evil Family Dedication

Less than a year ago, while praying for a certain individual, the spirit of the Lord revealed that this person had been dedicated to a local idol somewhere in Africa. This idol required sacrifices which the individual failed to deliver and as a result introduced more problems. This demonic contract was signed by parents without the knowledge of the individual. Except the Holy Spirit opens up your heart to know the specific prayers to pray, you may pray amiss. You need to pray to God to show you ancient secrets of your foundation.

Some naive parents have taken their children's names to demonic prophets in search of breakthroughs. This has caused havoc in the lives of many children and has hindered destiny. Some parents have bewitched their children, some have cursed the destinies and marriages of their children. Some parents have sexually defiled their children, some have swapped the destinies of their children.

Territorial Principalities

There is a very primitive town in Nigeria called Oyo. In the spiritual realm, Oyo is known to be the seat of the demonic. Regardless of how people preach, they are hardly receptive to the Word of God. There are so many spiritual atrocities committed in this town that they have closed the heavens over this town. Breakthrough is a very rare occurrence. For as many as have a linkage to that town, either by birth or marriage, you need to engage in strong spiritual warfare to cut off links to your demonic background. People who marry from this town find themselves under the yoke of the spirit of slavery. People coming from regions like this need deliverance from territorial strongholds

TACKLING FOUNDATIONAL DELIVERANCE

Foundational deliverance is sometimes one of the toughest to confront in spiritual warfare. The reason is that christians are often set back by sentiments and doubts despite being ensnared by evil practices. For some novice christians, they find it unbelieve that divination is rising against them from their households. Even when the Lord continues to reveal ancient secrets, they confide in their enemies. Only the power of the Holy Spirit can reveal and deliver completely. If faithfully and aggressively pray, victory will be granted to you by the Lord.

PRAYERS FOR DELIVERANCE FROM FOUNDATIONAL BONDAGE

- Confess and repent from all your sins.
- Build a life and relationship with the Lord.

Worship

- Build a worship altar to the Lord

Spend 12 minutes in worship before you say the prayers.

.

Personalize and meditate on the following Scriptures

"For no one can lay any foundation other than the one already laid, which is Jesus Christ" 1 Corinthians 3:11

"Therefore thus says the Lord GOD, "Behold, I am laying in Zion a stone, a tested stone, A costly cornerstone for the foundation, firmly placed. He who believes in it will not be disturbed" Isaiah 28:16

"storing up for themselves the treasure of a good foundation for the future, so that they may take hold of that which is life indeed" 1 Timothy 6:19

"Nevertheless, the firm foundation of God stands, having this seal, "The Lord knows those who are His," and, "Everyone who names the name of the Lord is to abstain from wickedness" 1 Timothy 2:19

"The stone which the builders rejected Has become the chief corner stone" Psalm 118:22

1. Father, thank you for the power in the blood of Jesus.
2. My father, visit the depth of my foundation and repair every rottenness in the name of Jesus.
3. Every victory in captivity - you are not what I am made for, my life rejects you, I am made for total victory, I receive victory and freedom out of captivity, in the name of Jesus.
4. Every network of oppressor arm stringing me for destruction, be destroyed by the fire of the Holy Spirit in

the name of Jesus

5. Every foundational anomaly that has plagued my destiny, be nullified in the name of Jesus.

6. Every evil inheritance from my parents, I sever ties with you by the power in the blood of Jesus.

7. Every curse that plagued my parents and is now in operation over my life, by the blood of Jesus, I silence you forever in the name of Jesus.

8. Every curse that has plagued me because of the sin of my ancestors and parents, by the blood of Jesus, I am set free in the name of Jesus.

9. Ancestral masquerades from my roots, from my place of birth & place of marriage, attacking my life in my dreams, be destroyed by the blazing sword of the Lord.

10. Every demonic carry over that has been walking against my destiny from generation to generation, today marks your end in my life in the name of Jesus.

11. Afflictions shall rise no more because I seal my prayers with the blood of Jesus and the fire of the Holy Spirit.

12. Glory and honor be to you Lord Jesus for answered prayers.

JOURNAL

12

QUENCHING THE FIRE OF REPROACH

Like a madman who throws firebrands, arrows, and death, Is the man who deceives his neighbor, And says, "I was only joking!" Proverbs 26:18-19

The enemy is a master at igniting the fire of reproach. The enemy ignites this fire, and sets up a campaign to disgrace the victim. The fire of reproach is the battle that is ruining lives and many of the lives that are being ruined continue to seek solace in their source of problems. The fire of reproach is fire lighted to discredit or scorn an individual behind their back. One the surface it looks like nothing is happening, but one who fires such arrows comes to the surface with a smile. The problem is that the fire of reproach if not combatted does great damage within a short while.

There was a sister who had been jobless for a number of years, even though she had numerous skills employers were looking for. Suddenly God opened a way, and she interviewed for a Director role in an organization. Out of all the candidates, she was the most preferred candidate. Everything seemed fine, until the CEO said "let me just do an informal background check and ask someone who attends the same church with her". The CEO called a friend who was a sister in the same church. The sister said: "she can do the job, the only problem is that she will bring a Jezebel spirit into your organization because she does not submit to leadership. That was the end of that offer. To make matters worse, the rejected sister was still asking her church sister, who just started the fire of reproach in her life, for advice.

The Scripture below gives insights into the war on reproach:

Where there is no wood, the fire goes out; And where there is no talebearer, strife ceases. As charcoal is to burning coals, and wood to fire, So is a contentious man to kindle strife. The words of a talebearer are like [asty trifles, And they go down into the inmost body. Fervent lips with a wicked heart Are like earthenware covered with silver dross. He who hates, disguises it with his lips, And lays up deceit within himself; When he speaks kindly, do not believe him, For there are seven abominations in his heart; Though his hatred is covered by deceit, His wickedness will be revealed before the assembly.
Proverbs 20:20-26

SITUATIONS WHERE THE FIRE OF REPROACH IS STARTED

Within the Family
In some families, one of the parents is the one

starting the fire of reproach. When some members of the family are not present, the parent brings up the matter of the absent family member, and begins reproach. This has scattered so many families and the reasons why many siblings no longer have healthy relationships are because either the father or mother started the fire of reproach , it was not detected on time and it cannot be contained any longer as the children had become wounded and hurt.

Within Friendships

There are friendships people get into that are worse than being in an enemy zone. Within such friendship, arrows of reproach fly from person to person and no one is exempted, as they all reproach each other behind. In such friendships, people just find out that though they pray hard, there is no light of the day or relevant breakthrough, it is because they are in the middle of reproach.

These are some examples. The situations

are endless. For some the husband is the one firing up reproach, for some it is the wife. For some it is the pastor, for some it is the best friend. The goal of reproach is to ruin godly opportunities and block all incoming blessings.

QUENCHING THE FIRE OF REPROACH

Many people make the mistake of going to confront individuals who have reproached them. This is wrong. When you do this, you take matters into your own hands. All you need to do is to forward the reports to God and request that a greater fire comes to fight on your behalf.

PRAYERS FOR QUENCHING THE FIRE OF REPROACH

- Confess and repent from all your sins.
- Build a life and relationship with the Lord.

Worship

- Build a worship altar to the Lord
- Spend 12 minutes in worship before you say the prayers.

Personalize and meditate on the following Scriptures

"Whoever digs a pit will fall into it,
And he who rolls a stone will have it roll back on him."
Psalm 26:27

1. Father, let every tongue spitting venom against me be consumed by the fire of the Holy Spirit in the name of Jesus.
2. Fire of reproach, lit against me, return to your senders in the name of Jesus.
3. Fire of reproach, lit against the works of

my hands, go right back upon your senders and multiply 7 folds upon the works of their hands in the name of Jesus.

4. Fire of reproach lit against my family by the workers of iniquity, let the Holy Spirit fire them back to senders in the name of Jesus.

5. Father, fight my cause against every lip discrediting your works in my life in the name of Jesus.

6. Father, arrest every lip projecting evil into my life in the name of Jesus.

7. Every mouth spitting forth evil against my person, to quench the glory of God in my life, father, send your arrows into such a mouth in the name of Jesus.

8. Let the words of the envious enemies against me return to them as an arrow in the name of Jesus.

9. Holy Spirit, return every venom of darkness coming out of the lips of the wicked back upon the wicked in the name of Jesus.

10. O God of vengeance, ignite numerous fires of reproach against every lip that ignited the fire of reproach against me in the name of Jesus.

11. Father, shut down the voice of the deceitful in the name of Jesus.

12. Take away the voice of the evil broadcaster in the name of Jesus.

13. Satanic advisers, be consumed by the fire of the Holy Spirit in the name of Jesus.

14. Father quench every fire and arrow of reproach in my foundation in the name of Jesus.

15. Flaming missiles of reproach fired at me, the voice of the redirect you right back at your senders 7 fold in the name of Jesus.

16. My Father, uproot reproach from the foundation of my life in the name of Jesus.

17. My Father, deliver me from the reproach of the adversaries in the name of Jesus.

18. Blood of Jesus, wipe out reproach completely from my bloodline in the name of Jesus.

19. Father, You are the One who pleads my cause, let wounds, dishonor and reproach be the portion of the one who fires reproach at me in the name of Jesus.

20. Father return reproach to the bosom of my enemies who have reproached your name in my life, in the name of Jesus.

21. Father, put an end to the snail race in my life in the name of Jesus

22. Powers that have turned my destiny into a foot mat and stepping stone, Father, let those powers catch fire in the name of Jesus.

23. I condemn the troublesome tongue,speaking trouble into my destiny, in the name of Jesus

24. I condemn every demonic tongue speaking against my destiny, in the name of Jesus.

25. I condemn all devouring tongues speaking evil into the core of my destiny, in the name of Jesus.

26.   I condemn every tongue that rises against me in the name of Jesus.

27. Every tongue speaking death and damnation and destruction against my destiny is condemned in the name of Jesus.

28. Every tongue that speaks damnation against my destiny is condemned in the name of Jesus.

29. Every tongue that devours is condemned in the name of Jesus.

30.   Every tongue spitting venom against me shall be consumed by the fire of the Holy Spirit

31. Lord, return the burning fire of reproach back to origins in the name of Jesus.

Ebenezer & Abigail Gabriels

JOURNAL

13

SECURING THE BORDERS OF YOUR LIFE FROM SATANIC ACCESS

Like a madman who throws firebrands, arrows, and death, Is
the man who deceives his neighbor,
And says, "I was only joking!"
Proverbs 26:18-19

God's Presence is a very secured area; so that any unclean thing does not get in there. Similarly, all individuals have their personal space, secured by God's angels. Ungodly access into people's personal space is the fastest way for the enemy to transport problems into your life.

Many people wonder why they remain in battles though they are believers, read the Word, and worship the Lord. Whenever your life is accessible to the satanic, there is a major problem of recurring and invisible battles, as it becomes hard to find out what the cause of the problem is, and the problem never goes away.

THE WORKINGS OF THE SATANIC ACCESS

1. To continue perpetual attack, the enemy needs constant access into your life. The enemy hires a satanic mercenary to access your life for penetration.
2. Mercenaries could be satanic people, satanic objects, satanic media, satanic or infested-teachings or your mouth.
3. Satanic access usually rides on vulnerability, bias, and emotions.
4. Satanic access is one of the reasons

people marry the wrong spouses.

SYMPTOMS THAT THERE IS A SATANIC ACCESSWAY IN YOUR LIFE

1. You are always attacking the wrong individuals that do not have your interest.
2. You are constantly attracting the wrong men or women in relationships.
3. You are always attracting people who do not add any value, but steal from you.
4. You find it hard to say no to demands you cannot meet.
5. Your life is a shadow of all the people around you and you have not come to hear God speak to you directly.

When you say close satanic access into your life, the enemy will try to return to negotiate. It is important to search out what type of access the enemy may have into your life, and close it by the fire of God and the blood of Jesus.

PRAYERS TO BARRICADE YOUR LIFE FROM SATANIC ACCESS

- Confess and repent from all your sins.
- Build a life and relationship with the Lord.

Worship
- Build a worship altar to the Lord
- Spend 12 minutes in worship before you say the prayers.

Personalize and meditate on the following Scriptures

Deliver me from my enemies, O my God;
Defend me from those who rise up against me.
Deliver me from the workers of iniquity,
And save me from bloodthirsty men.
For look, they lie in wait for my life;
The mighty gather against me,
Not for my transgression nor for my sin, O Lord.
They run and prepare themselves through no fault of mine.

Awake to help me, and behold!
You therefore, O Lord God of hosts, the God of Israel,
Awake to punish all the nations;
Do not be merciful to any wicked transgressors.
Psalm 59

1. Father, send that fire to barricade my life from all sort of satanic access in the name of Jesus.
2. Father, send your fire to quench every satanic desire, against me in the name of Jesus
3. Powers assigned me to chase me out of my inheritance, catch fire in the name of Jesus.
4. Satanic intruders will not eat from the altar of darkness in the name of Jesus
5. Their desire, thoughts and plans
6. No longer will access into my life be given to the workers of darkness
7. My foundation of my life receives fire for .
8. Fire from heaven, surround me for your protection in the name of Jesus.

9. Access of darkness into my destiny, be cut off by the fire of the Holy Spirit in the name of Jesus.

10. Father, reveal the faces of my enemies so that I will not aggregate my enemies around me in the name of Jesus.

11. Powers that have been covenanted to satan to wreck my life, Father, let the fire of the Holy Ghost rapidly consume such powers in the name of Jesus

12. Every raging power asking for payment in blood, I silence them in the name of Jesus.

13. Let the Lord Jesus be my advocate, in Jesus Name
    Every power requesting blood payment as a result of your bloodline, is consumed by the rapid fire of the Lord in the name of Jesus.

14. Every of my destiny that has been buried as a result of the works of the hand of my parents,come back to life in the name of Jesus.
    Every of my glory that has been buried

as a result of the works of the hands of ancestors, deliver me and let my glory come back to life

15. Every power that wants to hold me back where a satanic name was loaned to me, Lord tear those power in the name of Jesus.

16. Powers dictating how far I can go, be devoured by the fire of God in the name of God

17. Powers of witchcraft sending insects to devour my blessings, let the devouring fire of God burn you to ashes.

18. Witchcraft trackers placed in my life, catch fire in the name of Jesus.

19. Witchcraft ropes, tying me to witchcraft altars, let the consuming fire of God burn those ropes to ashes and I am set free in the name of Jesus.

20. Aggressive witchcraft battles from my bloodline affecting my destiny be devoured by the consuming fire of Yahweh in thy name of Jesus

21. Aggressive witchcraft battles that have its signature in my bones to afflict me unto desolation, be devoured by the consuming fire of Yahweh in the name of Jesus.

22. Witchcraft aggressive power that wants to ruin the works of my hand, fire from heaven consume them and tear in the name of Jesus.

23. Witchcraft power that wants the end of my life to end in nakedness and shame, we perish in the name of Jesus.

24. Every power that wants my work to become history is consumed by the rapid fire of the Lord.

25. Lord Jesus, withdraw satanic access from my life in the name of Jesus.

JOURNAL

14

DELIVERANCE FROM THE SPIRIT OF ERROR

When the spell of error is cast, this spell looks for people in their vulnerable times, at critical points in their lives when a breakthrough or promotion is near to discredit them. The spirit of error is a spirit that has long plagued God's children. This spirit seeks to hinder God's people from entering into the realm of perfection where God's eternal excellence is measured.

> *Woe to them! For they have gone in the way of Cain, have run greedily in the error of Balaam for profit, and perished in the rebellion of Korah"*
> *Jude 1:11 (NKJV)*

THE WORKINGS OF THE SPIRIT OF ERROR

The Spell of Error upon Leaders: The spell of error is cast by wicked powers to displace kings from their reign, knowing that some blunders can dethrone kings. This is why the Scripture notes that a king must not transgress in judgment.

The Spell of Error upon Marriages; When the The spell of error, when cast upon a spouse in marriage, they commit a blunder like sleeping with their domestic staff or getting into incestous relationships within a family.

The Spell of Error and the Day of Glory: This

spirit shows up on the day where God's glory is about to be revealed and then strikes. It is responsible for unthinkable error on special days, and must be rebuked way ahead

The Spell of Error and Destiny Helpers: This spirit can work against people when they are in close proximity with their destiny helpers. This spell pushes people to misbehave or wage war against their destiny helpers. At a time when people are supposed to be in submission to the Lord for the Lord to work through their destiny helpers, the spell of error pushes them into a rotten attitude. Example; a brother walks into a grocery store and picks up a fight with the grocer because he was told to go stand in the line, and he said, "I will make sure no customer will patronize this place again". The next week, he was at a job interview for the role of a Director of National Sales, he went through all the stages successfully, and at his final interview, it was face-to-face with the decision maker, the decision maker was the same grocer he dishonored. This is how the spell of error works against people when their destiny helpers are close by.

- The enemy uses the spirit of error to discredit
- The enemy uses the spirit of error to disqualify
- the enemy uses the spirit of error to destroy good works
- The enemy uses the spirit of error to taint the image.
- The enemy uses the spirit of error to displace.
- The enemy uses the spirit of error to term people as incompetent.
- The enemy uses the spirit of error to draw into unnecessary swiftness that brings destruction.

As you pray the following prayers, the Lord will deliver you the spirit of error.

PRAYERS OF DELIVERANCE FROM THE SPIRIT OF ERROR

- Confess and repent from all your sins.
- Build a life and relationship with the Lord.

Worship

- Build a worship altar to the Lord
- Spend 12 minutes in worship before you say the prayers.

.

Personalize and meditate on the following Scriptures

They are futile, a work of errors; In the time of their punishment they shall perish - Jeremiah 10:15 (NKJV)II Samuel 6:7 (NKJV)

Then the anger of the Lord was aroused against Uzzah, and God struck him there for his error; and he died there by the ark of God
II Samuel 6:7 (NKJV)

For our exhortation did not come from error or uncleanness,
nor was it in deceit
I Thessalonians 2:3 (NKJV)

We are of God. He who knows God hears us; he who is not of
God does not hear us. By this we know the spirit of truth and
the spirit of error.
I John 4:6 (NKJV)

1. I am delivered from the spirit of error in the name of

2. I shall not live my life in error, in the name of Jesus.

3. My life is delivered from carefully concealed traps of error, in the name of Jesus.

4. I will not be susceptible to the manifestations of error in the name of Jesus.

5. Uproot from my life, the manifestation of the spirit of error in the name of Jesus

6. Powers of the witch sent to bewitch me into error have failed woefully in the name of Jesus.

7. Satanic hands seeking to offer me a handshake of error is withered by the Finger of God in the name of Jesus.

8. Lord Jesus, deliver me friends from hell seeking to plant the seed of error in the name of Jesus.

9. Lord Jesus, deliver me from the powers of the psychics in the name of Jesus.

10. Lord Jesus, deliver me from the caterers from hell seeking to feed me with the food of error, in the name of Jesus.

11. My hands shall not be laced with error in the name of Jesus

12. Lord my Father, do not deliver me to the hands of the ungodly that they will not profane your glory in my life with error in the name of Jesus.

13. Do not deliver my destiny to the will of the spirit of error in the name of Jesus

14. Lord, do not allow the ungodly to violate my destiny with error in the name of Jesus

15. Lord, do not allow the wicked to violate my purpose in the name of Jesus.

16. Let not the glory of Israel concerning my life be violated with error in the name of Jesus.

17. Thou spirit of error, awaiting to manifest on the day of my appointment with destiny is destroyed by the consuming fire to the Lord.

18. Lord, execute your judgment against those standing in opposition against the move of God in the name of Jesus

19. Lord, measure out your judgment against the powers of error standing as a hindrance in the wheels of my destiny in the name of Jesus

20. Lord, measure out your judgment against the powers of error standing again the smooth running of my destiny in the name of Jesus

21. I shall not sing the Lord's song in error, in the name of Jesus.

22. Finger of God, remove all error planted as thorns in my life, in the name of Jesus

23. Finger of God, remove all the plantains of error that have been planted into my path, in the name of Jesus.

24. My hand is charged by the fire of the Holy Spirit, I shall no longer harvest from the tree of error in the name of Jesus.

25. My hand is charged by the fire of the Holy Spirit, the works of my hands shall no longer produce the corruption of error in the name of Jesus.

26.   My thought is charged by the word of God, therefore my thoughts are free from error in the name of Jesus

27. My lips are charged by the fire of the Holy Spirit, therefore my speech is free of error, in the name of Jesus.

28. My foot is anointed for the gospel of peace, therefore I shall no longer thread upon the pathway of error in the name of Jesus.

29. I receive realignment with the spirit of God's truth, in the name of Jesus.

30. No longer shall my life be in fellowship with the spirit of error in the name of Jesus.

31. The power of God that cannot fellowship with error is released upon my life, in the name of Jesus.

32. The perfection of God that does not condone error is released unto me in the name of Jesus

33. The anointing of God that shields from error is released over my life.

34. I shall no longer enter into the snare of error in the name of Jesus.

35. No longer will I be terned incompetent in my mind.

36. Arrows fired into my brain are uprooted and broken in the name of Jesus.

37. Voices of error speaking error into my destiny is shut down by the voice of God, in the name of Jesus.

38. Voices speaking to a part of me to manipulate me into error is shut down

by the voice of the Lord in the name of Jesus.

39. Lord Jesus, restore to me the symbol of your soundness in the name of Jesus.

40.   Lord Jesus, restore to me the symbol of perfection in the name of Jesus.

41. I receive the power of God's sound judgment in the name of Jesus.

42. I receive the soundness of mind, in the name of Jesus.

43. I receive the power of God's congruence, in the name of Jesus.

44. I receive the spirit of a sound mind, in the name of Jesus.

45. Let the grace of God that powers life be released upon my life in the name of Jesus.

46. Let the grace of the Lord for an error-free life be released.

JOURNAL

15

DESTROYING THE SCATTERING SPIRIT OF ABSALOM

Many builders are weary of building God's assignments entrusted in their care because the power of Absalom has taken over in the helms of affairs. Study the Scripture below to understand how the spirit of Absalom works

After this it happened that Absalom provided himself with chariots and horses, and fifty men to run before him. Now

*Absalom would rise early and stand beside the way to the gate.
So it was, whenever anyone who had a lawsuit came to the
king for a decision, that Absalom would call to him and say,
"What city are you from?" And he would say, "Your servant is
from such and such a tribe of Israel." Then Absalom would say
to him, "Look, your case is good and right; but there is no
deputy of the king to hear you." Moreover Absalom would say,
"Oh, that I were made judge in the land, and everyone who
has any suit or cause would come to me; then I would give him
justice." And so it was, whenever anyone came near to bow
down to him, that he would put out his hand and take him and
kiss him. 6In this manner Absalom acted toward all Israel who
came to the king for judgment. So Absalom stole the hearts of
the men of Israel.*

2 Samuel 15:1-6 NKJV

The spirit of Absalom has been sent out into the world; into marriages, families, businesses, groups, churches and everywhere possible.

THE WORKINGS OF THE SPIRIT OF ABSALOM

In Marriages: When the spirit of Absalom enters into a marriage, this spirit sets up its operation in the core of marriage to take over the marriage, and lure the husband or wife away. If this spirit succeeds, the husband just realizes his wife's heart is drawn to a strange man, or the husband's heart is drawn to the strange woman.

In Families: The spirit of Absalom seeks to take over the throne of a family, and run operations of a family to lure children or people out of the family.

In Businesses: In, the spirit of Absalom opens mini-business operations within a business to run its own business, and lure the souls of customers away. If allowed to thrive, the spirit of absalom lures away all the customers a business has, and displaces the business.

In Churches: In churches, the spirit of Absalom sets up its business station within the church, to lure souls out of God's presence.

In Government: The spirit of Absalom will seek to displace the current government by planning a coup.

THE NATURE OF THE SPIRIT OF ABSALOM

The spirit of Absalom works against establishments, or anything related to organization. This spirit scatters, brings desolations and displace the leader furthering God's purpose in a place. This spirit is usually brought alive against the works of the leadership in an establishment.

PRAYERS TO ANNIHILATE THE SCATTERING SPIRITS OF ABSALOM

- Confess and repent from all your sins.
- Build a life and relationship with the Lord.

Worship

- Build a worship altar to the Lord
- Spend 12 minutes in worship before you say the prayers.

Personalize and meditate on the following Scriptures

After this it happened that Absalom provided himself with chariots and horses, and fifty men to run before him. 2Now Absalom would rise early and stand beside the way to the gate. So it was, whenever anyone who had a lawsuit came to the king for a decision, that Absalom would call to him and say, "What city are you from?" And he would say, "Your servant is from such and such a tribe of Israel." 3Then Absalom would say to him, "Look, your case is good and right; but there is no deputy of the king to hear you." Moreover Absalom would say, "Oh, that I were made judge in the land, and everyone who has any suit or cause would come to me; then I would give him justice." And so it was, whenever anyone came near to bow down to him, that he would put out his hand and take him and kiss him. 6In this manner Absalom acted toward all Israel who came to the king for judgment. So Absalom stole the hearts of the men of Israel.

2 Samuel 15:1-6

1. Father, thank you for the power in the blood of Jesus.

2. Lord expose, disgrace and destroy the powers of the whispers sent to scatter my harvest in the name of Jesus.

3. Lord, measure desolation to the powers of the destroyers sowing the seed of destruction into the works of my hand, in the name of Jesus.

4. Fire of God, burn to ashes the works that the destroyer seeks to put together, as He delights in destroying others.

5. Finger of God, expose, ridicule and destroy, the plans of the scatterer sent to scatter the work I have labored for.

6. Finger of God, fish out all hidden Absalom that is orchestrating to ruin the work you have committed into my hands.

7. Finger of God, destroy the schemes of Absalom planning to open up satanic operations in the core of my life, in the name of Jesus.

8. Finger of God, destroy the schemes of Absalom planning to turn my helpers into my enemies in the name of Jesus.

9. Finger of God, expose the invisible ploys of Absalom hiding in plain sight to afflict me, in the name of Jesus.

10. Finger of God, destroy the organization of Absalom coming together to scatter God's purpose in my life, in the name of Jesus.

11. Lord Jesus, visit the prying eyes of Absalom with confusion in the name of Jesus.

12. Thou judgment of God, consume upon the powers of absalom using the tool of satanic pity to work against my purpose in the name of Jesus.

13. Thou judgment of God, consume the powers and works of Absalom deceiving souls and gathering pity to scatter God's

purpose in my life, in the name of Jesus.

14. Thou consuming fire of the Lord, visit for utter destruction all satanic offices of Absalom set up in the front door of my God-given purpose, in the name of Jesus.

15. Thou consuming fire of the Lord, visit for utter destruction all satanic offices of Absalom set up in the front door of my God-given purpose, in the name of Jesus.

16. Thou consuming fire of the Lord, visit for utter destruction all satanic offices of Absalom set up in the parking lot my God-given purpose, in the name of Jesus.

17. Thou consuming fire of the Lord, visit for utter destruction all satanic devices of Absalom being used to dismantle my God-given organization, in the name of Jesus.

18. Thou garment of desolation, hear the Word of God, find out all desolators firing the arrows of desolation into my life, and destroy their full covering in the name of Jesus.

19. All devouring tongue of Absalom,

waging the war of words against my destiny shall be cut off by the battle ax of the Lord, in the name of Jesus

20. The plans of Absalom to plunder my destiny have failed woefully, in the name of Jesus.

21. The schemes of Absalom, to rise early to lay low at the gates of my destiny, are destroyed in the name of Jesus.

22. The powers of Absalom which seek to cast the shadow of doubt upon my God-given decisions are destroyed in the name of Jesus.

23. Powers of Absalom which seek to undo God's completed works through me are cast into eternal desolation, in the name of Jesus.

24. Let the powers of darkness seeking to gather as I scattered be disgraced, in the name of Jesus.

25. Thou satanic whisperer, seeking to whisper evil into the soul of my harvest is consumed by the rapid fire of the Lord.

26. Thou unrepentant detractor, seeking to create confusion in the midst of peace is disenfranchised by the consuming fire of the Lord.

27. Powers specializing in scattering the harvest of others is consumed by the rapid fire of the Lord.

JOURNAL

16

DELIVERANCE FROM DESECRATING POWERS

Desecrating powers seek to pollute the goodness of God in people's lives. Desecrating spirits are spirits that ruin goodness, and replace it with filthiness.

Dead flies putrefy the perfumer's ointment, And cause it to give off a foul odor; So does a little folly to one respected for wisdom and honor.

Ecclesiastes 10:1

THE WORKINGS OF THE SPIRIT OF DESECRATION

1. When you are trying to get closer to God, and the sinner friend male or female drags you back with the chains of iniquity.
2. When the enemy comes to plant the seed of destruction in the midst of plenty.
3. When the enemy comes to pull down false accusations and lies.
4. These powers plant the seeds of demonic words into the souls of people to corrupt.
5. When the enemy comes to pollute in order to introduce shame or sorrow to your victory.
6. When the enemy sneaks in to corrupt the good works you are doing.

PRAYERS TO DESTROY DESECRATING SPIRITS

- Confess and repent from all your sins.
- Build a life and relationship with the Lord.

Worship

- Build a worship altar to the Lord
- Spend 12 minutes in worship before you say the prayers.

Personalize and meditate on the following Scriptures

They shall not profane the holy offerings of the children of Israel, which they offer to the Lord, 16or allow them to bear the guilt of trespass when they eat their holy offerings; for I the Lord sanctify them.' "
Leviticus 22:15

1. Powers of the desecrator is destroyed over my life in the name of Jesus
2. Powers planning to bring dung upon

God's glory in my life is disgraced in the name of Jesus.

3. Powers seeking to scatter the works of my hand are destroyed in the name of Jesus.

4. Powers seeking to ridicule God's calling upon my life is disgraced by the rapid fire of the Lord in the name of Jesus.

5. Thou tongue of the wicked against my glory, be consumed by the rapid fire of God, in the name of Jesus.

6. Powers running satanic campaigns against my destiny is consumed by the rapid fire of the Lord in the name of Jesus.

7. Powers spreading false reports to hinder my destiny is consumed by the rapid fire of the Lord in the name of Jesus.

8. Powers seeking to serve me dung is consumed by the rapid fire of the Lord in the name of Jesus.

9. Powers seeking to place dung in the front yard of my destiny is consumed by the rapid fire of the Lord in the name of

Jesus.

10. Powers targeting my day of joy to bring dung at the moment of joy are consumed by the rapid fire of God in the name of Jesus.

11. The rod of dishonor shall not locate me in the name of Jesus.

12. Promote me Lord, above reproach in the name of Jesus.

13. My name shall no longer be associated with rottenness in the name of Jesus.

14. The desecrator shall be caught in the traps it has set, in the name of Jesus.

17

DELIVERANCE FROM DESECRATING POWERS

Desecrating powers seek to pollute the goodness of God in people's lives. Desecrating spirits are spirits that ruin goodness, and replace it with filthiness.

15. Lord, give me the power for to eat
16. Lord Jesus, endow me with the power to partake from my toil

17. Lord Jesus, endow me with the power to partake from the works I have done.

18. Lord Jesus, let your rapid fire consume powers seeking to afflict me out of the works of my hand.

19. Lord Jesus, uproot the powers seeking to replace me in my place of assignment.

20. Lord Jesus, let your rapid fire consume the powers seeking to use me as a stepping stone in the name of Jesus.

21. Lord Jesus, consume the evil afflictors seeking to displace me from my marriage.

22. Lord Jesus, let your rapid fire consume the powers seeking to use me as a staircase in the name of Jesus.

SPECIAL CASES BLOOD DELIVERANCE RECOMMENDATION

If your blood has been taken over by darkness, or the enemy has penetrated your blood, and your blood is fighting against you.

Deliverance Study Recommendations:

The Deeper Mysteries of the Blood

The Ministry of Water

SPECIAL CASES DELIVERANCE RECOMMENDATION

If you have been wounded under the dark altars, false altars, or under the anointing of sorcerers the pulpit.

If you have been sexually abused by ministers, and are not sure where your virtues are, or if your destiny has been traded. The hands of the Lord will deliver you, cleanse you, and purify you for His use, so you can fulfill your assignment on here.

Personal Deliverance Study Recommendations:

- Uncursed for Foundational Deliverance
- Deeper Mysteries of the Blood
- War of Altars
- Unprofaned Purpose
- Technical Prayers

Cant find these books on Amazon?

- Email <u>hello@ebenezergabriels.org</u> for other ordering information.

ABOUT THE AUTHORS

About the Authors

Ebenezer Gabriels is an Innovator. Media Apostle of the Lord Jesus, the Apostle of Worship, Innovation Leader, Prophetic Leader, Revivalist, and a Computer Scientist who has brought heaven's solutions into Financial markets, Technology, and Government with his computational gifts. Apostle Gabriels is anointed as a Prophetic Leader of nations with the mantle of healing, worship music, national deliverance, foundational deliverance, complex problem-solving, and building Yahweh's worship altars.

Abigail Ebenezer-Gabriels, a Teacher, Business Leader, Strategy and Policy Expert, Executive Co-Founder at the Ebenezer Gabriels Teacher, Worshiper, and Multi-disciplinary leader in Business, Technology, Education, and Development. Blessed with prophetic teaching abilities with the anointing to unveil the mysteries in the Word of God. She is a Multi-specialty Keynote Speaker, with a special anointing to explain Heaven's ordinances on earth.

Ebenezer Gabriels & Abigail Ebenezer-Gabriels are married, and building worship altars for the Lord across industries.

**Ebenezer
Gabriels
ministries**

About Ebenezer Gabriels

At Ebenezer Gabriels Ministries (EGM), we fulfill the mandate of building worship altars by sharing the story of the most expensive worship ever offered by Jesus Christ, the Son of God and dispersing the aroma of the knowledge of Jesus Christ to the ends of the world.

Ebenezer Gabriels Publishing delivers biblically grounded learning experiences that prepare audiences for launch into their prophetic calling. We create educational content and deliver in innovative ways through online classrooms, apps, audio, and prints to enhance the experience of each audience as they are filled with the aroma of Christ knowledge and thrive in their worship journey.

CONTACT

hello@ebenezergabriels.org
www.ebenezergabriels.org

Other Books

Other Books by Ebenezer and Abigail Gabriels

Worship

Worship is Expensive

War of Altars

Business and Purpose

Unprofaned Purpose for Business

Elements of Time

Spirit of Teams

Kids

Activating my Prophetic Senses for Kids

Bree Learns about Processes

Places we went - Jerusalem

The Excellent Spirit of Daniel

The Birth of a King

Places we went - Uganda

Marriage

Heaven's Gate way to a Blissful marriage for Him

Heaven's Gateway to a Blissful marriage for Her

Deliverance from the Yokes of Marital Ignorance

Pulling Down the Strongholds of Evil Participants in Marriage

Prophetic

The Prophetic System

Activating Your Prophetic Senses

Dreams and Divine Interpretations

Relationships (singles)

Heaven's Compass for Cultivating a Blissful Pre-Marital
Atmosphere for Her

Heaven's Compass for Cultivating a Blissful Pre-Marital
Atmosphere for Him

Deliverance

Uncursed

Deliverance from the Yoke of Accursed Names

Deliverance from the Curse of Vashti

Deliverance from the Yoke of Incest

Deliverance from the Wrong Family Tree

Principles of Prophetic Deliverance

Mind

Deliverance from the Yokes Deep Mysteries of Creation
in the Realms of Thoughts, Imaginations and Words

Spiritual War and Prayers

Blazing Sword of the Lord

Rapid Fire

The Big Process called Yoke

Deliverance of the Snares of the Fowler

The only Fire that Extinguishes Witchcraft

No longer Fugitives of the Earth

Subduers of the Earth

Prayers of the Decade

Manifold Mysteries of Water

Growth and Advancing in Faith

Men: Called out of the Dunghill

Women: Bearers of Faith

New Beginnings in Christ

Wisdom my Companion

Deeper Mysteries of the Blood

Nations and intercessions

The Scroll and the Seal

America: The Past, the Present and the Next Chapter

Herod: The Church and Nigeria

Prophetic Insights into the Year

21 Weapons of Survival for 2021

2022 Meet the God Who Saves Blesses Shepherds and Carries

Soul

Deeper Mysteries of the Soul (English, Spanish, Arabic and Chinese)

Unmute my Soul

Uncursed Series

The Spiritually Intelligent Mother

Read from the Ebenezer Gabriels Reading Room on Ebenezer Gabriels Books

SCAN ME

Read from the Ebenezer Gabriels Prophecy Room

Read from the Ebenezer Gabriels Worship

Discipleship